MIDWEST WEEKENDS

MIDWEST WEEKENDS

Memorable Getaways
in the Upper Midwest

by Beth Gauper

St. Paul Pioneer Press

ANDREWS AND McMEEL
A Universal Press Syndicate Company
Kansas City

to Eric
with love and admiration

MIDWEST WEEKENDS: Memorable Getaways in the Upper Midwest
© 1996 St. Paul Pioneer Press. All rights reserved. Printed in the
United States of America. No part of this book may be used or reproduced in any manner whatsoever without the written permis-
sion of Andrews and McMeel except in the case of reprints in the
context of reviews. For information, write Andrews and McMeel,
a Universal Press Syndicate Company, 4900 Main Street, Kansas
City, Missouri 64112.

Book designer: Diane Marshall

Additional copies of this book may be ordered by calling (800)
642-6480.

Library of Congress Cataloging-in-Publication Data

Gauper, Beth.
    Midwest Weekends : memorable getaways in the Upper Midwest /
        by Beth Gauper.
            p.   cm.
    Includes index.
    ISBN 0-8362-1444-7 (pbk.)
    1. Middle West—Guidebooks.   I. Title.
    F350.3.G38   1996
    917.704'33—dc20
                                                96-5195
                                                CIP

Contents

CANADA

Winnipeg

MINNESOTA

Ely
Grand Marais
Lutsen
Finland

Lake
Superior

Itasca   Walker
Callaway

Two Harbors
Duluth   Bayfield
Superior   Ashland
Cable
Hinckley   Hayward

NORTH

DAKOTA

WISCONSIN

SOUTH

DAKOTA

Chetek
Osceola
Spicer   Stillwater
Granite   Twin   Hudson   Menomonie
Falls   Cities   Red   Eau Claire
Redwood Falls   Excelsior   Wing   Maiden Rock
Northfield   Stockholm
DeSmet   Walnut   New   Pepin
Grove   Ulm   Faribault   Wabasha
Mankato   Lanesboro   Trempealeau
Preston   La   Sparta
Pipestone   Albert Lea   Harmony   Crosse   Wisconsin Dells
Lansing   Ontario   Baraboo
Decorah   Spring   Mount
Prairie du   Green   Horeb   Madison
Marquette   Chiee
McGregor   Mineral   New Glarus
Guttenberg   Point
Dubuque   Galena

IOWA

Amana
Iowa
City
Des
Moines   Kalona   ILLINOIS

N

Introduction

The Upper Midwest of this book is a wonderful place for explorers. Bisected by the Mississippi River, bordered by unruly Lake Superior and stamped with ancient ridges and valleys, it's full of unexpected contours and hidden niches.

It's also home to many delightful small towns and people whose down-to-earth friendliness quickly endears them to visitors.

I've been lucky to explore this varied terrain in my work as Midwest Weekends columnist for the *St. Paul Pioneer Press*. In each of these columns, which I now present as a guidebook, I have tried to do two things: to convey a sense of the place, and also to provide the means to get to know it better.

So I've included lots of phone numbers, schedules and fee information, and they're as up-to-date as I could make them. Yet it always pays to call before going; even if, for example, the date of a festival hasn't changed, you might pick up some useful tip about visiting it. And tourism groups happily send out piles of information, which give more detail than I can.

Though I often recommend that people travel midweek— it's cheaper, more relaxing, and easier to be spontaneous—the best way to get to know a town is during its special events. I

have noted which ones are especially popular, and for these it's smart to plan up to a year ahead. Even ordinary summer and fall weekends at popular destinations—Bayfield, Lanesboro, the North Shore—book up early; spring is a good time to reserve.

If there is one piece of advice I can offer about traveling in this region, it is to strike up conversations with people along the way; you will be richly rewarded. Also, carry a very good map. I never travel without a De-Lorme Atlas and Gazetteer, which allows me to roam far from the beaten path.

It is, unfortunately, necessary to state that the *Pioneer Press* paid for all my lodgings, meals and admissions, and that it was never at the behest of an inn keeper or chamber of commerce that I visited. Many travel guidebooks today are little more than paid advertising; this is not one of them, and I have tried at all times to see the region as an ordinary travel consumer does.

If you find that one of your favorite places is not included in this book, it's probably because I haven't gotten to it yet. I hope the day never comes when I've explored every interesting corner of this area, and I don't expect it will; there are too many of them. Meanwhile, happy travels.

Beth Gauper
March 1996

1 DULUTH AND THE NORTH SHORE

Duluth

In summer, a magnet for boat watchers

The *Lee Tregurtha* is late making its way through the Duluth boat canal, and Beth Duncan is starting to get heat from a throng of impatient boat watchers.

"What's it doing, just hanging around out there? Why doesn't it come in?" they ask, buzzing around her desk. Patiently, the Army Corps of Engineers employee explains: There already are two ships at the docks the *Tregurtha* needs to go to, and it's doing all it can do, which is to go in circles out on Lake Superior and wait.

"It's a very busy day," she offers, to which an older woman waspishly replies, "It doesn't look like it to me; of course, I'm thinking back to when I grew up here."

Yes, it's true: Duluth, while still the No. 1 shipping port on the Great Lakes, does not have the levels of traffic it once had. But the boats that do come are much bigger, and watching them is addictive.

"When they're coming, it's a magnet," Duncan says with a smile. "Cars drive up and all the people come running through the parking lot; it's comical."

I arrived in Canal Park on a Friday afternoon in June and immediately hit the boat-watcher's jackpot. At 4:40, bells began to ring, and the Aerial Lift Bridge began to rise. A few minutes later, the *Adam Cornelius* from Ohio pushed through the canal, making its dark waters heave as if it were a fat man on a waterbed.

"The *Adam E. Cornelius* is 680 feet in length and was built in 1973 in Toledo," intoned an amplified voice from inside the Marine Museum. "It will take on a load of taconite pellets." Then, at the dot of 5, the rust-colored hull of the *Kinsman Enterprise* approached, and at 5:30, the *Federal Vibeke* out of Oslo, Norway, departed, followed closely by a dozen yachts and sailboats.

The massive ore boats going in and out of Duluth Harbor are really something to see. But they're no longer the only thing to watch along the lakefront.

Nowadays, the lakefront has a carnival atmosphere. Horses drawing carriages clop along a dirt path, in tandem with in-line skaters on asphalt and walkers on a boardwalk. Lovers sit on benches, and sea gulls, as aggressive as winged monkeys but a lot noisier, troll for popcorn. New hotels sit a stone's throw from the Lift Bridge, across from galleries, shops, cafes and some of the many sprightly sculptures that now line the shore.

I set off along the Lake Walk, past the site of Duluth's first harbor, dashed to ruins by the lake, and near the rail tracks that take tourists up to Two Harbors. The smell of barbecued ribs wafts down from Pickwick's, an old standby in the renovated Fitger's complex of shops, restaurants and an inn.

Today, Lake Walk extends nearly three miles, far past Fitger's. I walk past thousands of freshly planted azaleas, day lilies and French lilacs, and marvel at the expenditure; the lakefront, shabby and neglected for so many years, has made a miraculous turnaround.

Leif Erikson Park is another revelation, a bowl of green with a band pavilion flanked by stone towers with shingled cone tops. A shed houses a 42-foot replica of a Viking ship, used in 1926 by four Norwegian sailors to re-create the trans-Atlantic route taken by Leif Erikson in 997.

Late into the evening, people still are streaming in and out of DeWitt-Seitz Marketplace and Grandma's restaurants. At 11 P.M., the area, lit by pink, blue and red neon, is still busy.

The next morning, I remember that the *Fred R. White Jr.* is due at 9, and run over to the canal. But it slipped in at 8:10; the next scheduled arrival is at noon.

The Marine Museum is a great place to bide time. Along with a replica of a 1920 ship's pilothouse are three re-created cabins from an 1870s schooner, a 1905 passenger steamer and a 1910 freighter, furnished with plaster figures and items salvaged from real ships. At the press of a button, a story is given on tape. In the case of the schooner, it takes the form of a letter, written to "My dear boy" during a winter nor'easter and advising the recipient to stay in his present job because sailing is "a regular dog's life."

So much for romanticism. I give up on ore boats and walk

down Canal Park Drive, where I pick up a cappuccino at the Blue Note Cafe and pass a series of shops and outfitters in a restored 1945 brick warehouse. Suddenly, a handsome man on a horse emerges, says a crisp "Good morning" and steps away down the sidewalk. I look at the sign over the door: Duluth Mounted Police.

Yes, it's Duluth. But I'm still pinching myself.

❂ TRIP TIPS: Duluth Lakefront

- **Shipping:** The Boat Watcher's Hotline is (218) 722-6489. The Marine Museum gives daily programs in July and August; call (218) 727-2497.

- **Accommodations:** For summer stays, reserve as early as possible. In Canal Park are the handsome Comfort Suites, (218) 727-1378 and (800) 221-2222, $65–$149 depending on season, and the new, three-story Inn on Lake Superior, $74–$159, (218) 726-1111 and (888) 668-4352 (toll-free).
  Fitger's Inn, (800) 726-2982, also overlooks the lake. Rooms and suites go for $72–$295.

- **Restaurants:** The Lake Avenue Cafe, (218) 722-2355, in the Dewitt-Seitz Marketplace, has excellent food and friendly service; Grandma's, (218) 727-4192, is more family-oriented, with a broad menu and convivial atmosphere.

- **Excursions:** From May through October, the North Shore Scenic Railroad offers daily excursions, some with dinners. Call (218) 722-1273. Harbor cruises on the Vista fleet, some with meals, are given several times a day; call (218) 722-6218.

- **Museums:** The Depot, (218) 727-8025, houses the Duluth Children's Museum, Lake Superior Museum of Transportation (including old locomotives), Duluth Art Institute and St. Louis Country Historical Society.

- **Events:** Grandma's Marathon generally is on the third Saturday of June. A Viking Festival in Leif Erikson Park is held in mid-July. The Bayfront Blues Festival is on the second weekend in August.
  The John Beargrease Sled Dog Marathon is held the second or third week of January; call (218) 722-7631.
  Summer concerts are held at Bayfront Park Friday evenings from late May through August; family entertainment is offered Saturdays at noon at nearby Playfront Park, which has a wonderful playground.

- **Information**: (800) 438-5884, or (218) 722-4011.

Two Harbors

A still-working port town with lots of memories

Most people know Two Harbors only by its spine, U.S. Highway 61, where a long gantlet of boutiques, bait shops and hamburger joints tries to reel in tourists speeding up the North Shore.

Yes, Two Harbors is the last place to get a Big Mac before Canada. But there are other, better reasons to stop there. When my family and I finally turned off the highway, we found the real Two Harbors, which has a downtown gussied up by old-time facades, five museums and a harbor that, since 1884, has started Iron Range ore on its voyage to eastern steel mills.

Ore boats still pull into Agate Bay's towering docks nearly every day for loads of taconite, still brought in by rail on the Duluth, Misabe and Iron Range line. A smaller boat operates from this bay, ferrying its passengers past Silver Cliff, Encampment Island and Split Rock Lighthouse to Beaver Bay and back. We bought tickets for the *Grampa Woo*—half-price due to heavy fog—but its personable captain, Dana Kollars, insisted on giving us a harbor tour for free.

"It's such a beautiful cruise," he said. "You'll have to come back later in the summer."

We chugged out and, in half an hour, got a primer on Agate Bay, which, with neighboring Burlington Bay, gives the town its name. Kollars' son, Clinton, pointed out now-empty Whiskey Row, where Great Lakes sailors could have a good time, and hopped onto the footing of a dock to fetch us a handful of dusty red taconite pellets. His father recounted the days of wooden schooners—the breakwater is built over the stern of one, the *Samuel P. Ely,* wrecked in 1896—when a boat had to labor for a year to carry what a modern ore boat can in one trip.

And we saw the picturesque *Edna G.,* the last coal-powered tug on the Great Lakes that still works, though she's now retired. Mostly, she pulled boats during her long career, 1896 to 1981, but she also rescued sailors during such wicked times as November 1905, when 30 boats were crippled in storms along the North Shore.

At the edge of the new DNR public boat landing, the last working lighthouse on the North Shore was flashing, electronically controlled from Duluth. The Lighthouse Point and Harbor Museum is one of four museums run by the Lake County Historical Society; it's housed in the old Depot, which greets excursion trains from Duluth.

Outside the Depot were parked two massive steam locomotives, one of them weighing more than a million pounds. Inside were photographic glimpses of the town's colorful history: legendary musher John Beargrease with his wife and four kids; a local judge as a baby in an Ojibwe cradleboard; a moose team pulling a sleigh; hopeful miners during the Lake Vermilion gold rush of 1865–68.

Another era is covered two blocks away at the private Great Lakes Fur Trade Museum. Proprietor Caroline Miller gave the children pieces of buckskin and showed off some of the many treasures unearthed by her husband, Wad, a voyageur hobbyist who runs the antique mall in the basement. There was a French copper kettle, much-patched, from the 1600s; a powderhorn marked "Friedrich Schwatz, His Horn 1771 Febr."; plus a beaver-felt hat, a European fad that prompted the first exploitation of the American interior.

On the way to our rented cabin north of town, we searched in vain for the office of my husband's great-uncle Art, a Two Harbors lawyer who, to my husband's great regret, was not the attorney who co-founded 3M here in 1902; that man's office is now the 3M/Dwan Museum, which tells how a bungled search for an abrasive mineral led to the huge corporation.

We picked up a fried-chicken dinner at Miller's Cafe and headed six miles north of town, turning after the new Silver Cliff tunnel at Halcyon Harbor. There, we dismissed our last illusion—that Two Harbors is not yet the *real* North Shore.

Halcyon Harbor is known for its 1930s Cliff House, which juts over the lake and has entertained such guests as Sinclair Lewis and Milton Berle. But I remember it for the curving, pebbled beach 30 feet below, reached by a swinging staircase. We built a fire behind a huge boulder at the foot of the cliff and watched the crashing waves as our children safely played in the sea of smooth pebbles. No sign of civilization marred the view; we could see only rock, trees and lake.

Sure, there are lots of scenic points farther north, and perhaps the isolation is more splendid there. Even so, we don't whiz by Two Harbors anymore.

❂ TRIP TIPS: Two Harbors

- **Events:** Heritage Days is on the second weekend in July.

  The Two Harbors Folk Festival is on the third weekend in July.

  On Nov. 10, the anniversary of the 1975 sinking of the ore boat Edmund Fitzgerald, the retired Split Rock Lighthouse, 19 miles north, lights its beacon and holds programs; (218) 226-4372.
- **Museums:** The Lake County Historical Society offers tours and sells tickets at the Depot, $7 for all four of the museums it runs: The Edna G., lighthouse, 3M and historical museum.
- *Grampa Woo* **cruises:** Various excursions between Two Harbors and Tettegouche State Park, Memorial Day weekend through October. Cost of the trips, 1½ to 2 hours, is $18, $8 children, $49 families. Call (218) 226-4100. Tickets are sold at the Depot.
- **Superior Hiking Trail:** For maps and information about shuttles, stop at the Superior Hiking Trail Association's office and store in a Victorian house at 731 Highway 61 (Seventh Avenue), open year-round. Call (218) 834-2700.
- **Accommodations:** Halcyon Harbor, four large cabins and a studio, all with fireplaces, $75–$120. Call (218) 834-2030.

  Bryan House B&B, 1905 bungalow. Three rooms, $60–$70. Call (800) 950-4797 or (218) 834-2950.

  Superior Shores, one mile north, is a large complex of attractive hotel rooms, studios, suites and townhouses, with two outdoor pools, one indoor pool, two saunas, a whirlpool, tennis courts, and restaurant with patio, $49 for a midweek hotel room in the shoulder season to $269 for a three-bedroom townhouse on a summer weekend. The townhouses are on the lake; the other units aren't, but most have views. New management says it began correcting service and design problems in 1995; call (800) 242-1988.

  Cove Point Lodge, 23 miles north, is an attractive new 45-room lodge that is positioned well for hikers and cross-country skiers; it's 10 miles or less from Gooseberry, Split Rock and Tettegouche state parks. Rates are $55–$140; call (800) 598-3221.
- **Information:** Two Harbors chamber, (800) 777-7384 or (218) 834-2600.

Wolf Ridge
A beautiful campus high above Lake Superior

There's a wooded enclave on the North Shore where small miracles happen.

The metal handle of a spigot becomes captivating. A tree stump holds deeper meaning. On this weekend, it was all thanks to the magical eye of Doug Beasley.

Every week during the school year, the nonprofit Wolf Ridge Environmental Learning Center near Finland is home to 230 lucky schoolchildren, who come from all over the state with their teachers to ski, hike, canoe and learn about nature at the $6 million campus high above Lake Superior, which opened in 1988. On weekends, adults get a turn.

When I went up, the place was a beehive of creativity. Grand Marais woodcut artist Betsy Bowen had a roomful of women raptly chiseling blocks of pine. Students from Range Technical College were making pysanky, tracing Ukrainian designs on eggs with hot wax.

In my "Zen and the Art of Photography" group, professional photographer Doug Beasley had his hands full training four pairs of eyes to look beyond pretty sunsets and panoramas. "A photo is not just a visual diary; it should show what it felt like to be there," he told us earnestly. "You have to open yourself up visually, so the photo opportunities will present themselves. Sometimes, you can walk on a mountaintop and not see anything. Other times, you walk in an alley and see pictures everywhere. A lot of it is where we are inside."

From Friday evening to Sunday afternoon, Beasley showed us techniques, urged us to ignore the rules, even served as subject: When he and his studio manager, Dani Werner, returned from a quiet canoe glide around Wolf Lake, they were ambushed by students. "Four hundred miles from the St. Lawrence and we run into paparazzi," he said good-naturedly.

The 1,400 acres of Wolf Ridge, which include two lakes, two gentle mountains and a river, are like a candy store for photographers. On Saturday morning, sent off with orders to shoot close-ups, another student and I set off through a birch-tree forest toward the beaver ponds on Sawmill Creek. The morning was still and gray, but there was color everywhere: the luminous chartreuse of lichen, the bright white of tree fungus, the subtle peach underskin of the birches. Inspired, we snapped away.

But as we were skipping about in the aesthetic feast of forests and wetlands, our instructor was simply walking around outside the education building. The 36 black-and-white exposures Beasley shot on instant Polapan slide film, which he showed us when we got back, were a revelation. The images weren't exactly of anything, but they were beautiful: the handles of a push lawn mower. Rope around a pole. Two crossed twigs. The handle of a spigot made to look like a space-age marigold.

It was an instant lesson on the power of the inner eye.

In the evening, everyone gathered in the auditorium for that Saturday's program, "Frozen Beans on a Tin Plate: An Evening With a Logging Camp Cook." The scene: 4:30 A.M. on a cold northern Minnesota day in 1901. While stirring a bowl of dough, Terry McLaughlin portrayed a cranky camp cook ("I've got just five rules: Come in. Sit down. Shut up. Eat. Get out") and painted a fascinating portrait of the dangerous, uncomfortable life of loggers, using slides of old photographs to illustrate. McLaughlin, who in real life is director of naturalist training, even led us in an old logging song, revealing a beautiful soprano voice and an easy touch on the guitar.

Talent and beauty are everywhere at Wolf Ridge. Scratch a surface, and you may find something surprising.

✿ TRIP TIPS: Wolf Ridge Environmental Center

- **Getting there:** The center is north of Silver Bay, five miles west of Highway 61 near Finland.
- **Programs:** Among the most popular programs are dog-sledding, drum-making, hiking, birding and photography, and fly-fishing and Mother Earth spirituality nearly always have waiting lists. Family weekends are held each fall and spring; in winter, the week between Christmas and New Year's also is for families. In summer, camps are held for children 9–18.
- Cost generally is $160. Groups of 10 or more can plan their own weekend programs. Accommodations are in small, plain dormitory rooms with bunk beds; meals are eaten cafeteria-style.

Lutsen
The North Shore's Gold Coast

About two-thirds of the way up the North Shore is a rugged stretch of shoreline, homesteaded in 1885 by Swedish immigrant Charles Axel Nelson. Nelson started a hunting and fishing camp, the North Shore's first resort, on his land, and a community developed called Lutsen. His descendants developed the hills around it into a ski area and even produced Olympic alpine medalist Cindy Nelson, but started selling it all off in the 1980s.

Today, the area around Lutsen is known as the Gold Coast, and the ranks of hunters and fishermen have thinned. Now, visitors to Lutsen come for:

• Skiing at Lutsen Mountains, the Midwest's largest ski resort, with its 1,000-foot vertical drops and four mountains.

• Mountain biking, in which a gondola and chairlift carry bikers to the top of Moose and Mystery mountains for the plunge down along more than 50 kilometers of trails.

• Golfing at Superior National Golf Course, with its great vistas of Lake Superior.

• Hiking along the Superior Hiking Trail, one of the nation's longest and best.

• Fall colors up the nearby Caribou and Sawbill trails and at Temperance and Cascade state parks along the shore.

Once, visitors had little choice in lodgings. But a 1990s construction boom resulted in many more rooms, many with such luxuries as fireplaces and whirlpools. They're most expensive on peak ski-season weekends; summer is a little cheaper. During the slow seasons, late October to Thanksgiving and April to mid-May, prices generally are cut in half. There's usually good skiing from Thanksgiving to mid-December, but prices are not yet at peak; during all seasons, midweek is much cheaper. All of the inns offer ski packages that reduce room costs considerably.

• Lutsen Resort & Sea Villas, on Nelson's original site, has four types of lodgings. The two-bedroom log cabins, up the hill from the lodge, are new and very popular. The look is Ma and Pa Ingalls outfitted by Eddie Bauer—woodburning stoves, wool-like rugs on shiny wood floors, quilts, handmade furniture, plus modern kitchens and bathrooms.

The cabins are beautiful, but parents of small children won't like their spot at the top of a steep dropoff to Lake Superior. On peak ski-season weekends, they rent for $239.

The Sea Villas, $179–$249, surrounded by woods and right at the edge of the lake, were built in the 1970s and are privately owned condos, which means furnishings are the luck of the draw. But the location, three miles south of the lodge, is lovely, and there's a playground for children.

In the winter, cozy rooms in the 1952 lodge go for $99–$129. Sure, they're a little dowdy, and the ceilings are low, but staying in one means you can walk to the pool and sauna complex and for a drink in the lobby, which, with its big stone hearth, polished leather chairs and picture windows overlooking the lake, is one of the most inviting places in Minnesota. The big drawback for families is the expense of eating in the lodge's restaurant, where dinner entrees are a bit steep.

The Cliff House, near the lodge, has views of the lake and a low price of $69–$89. Avoid the first-floor rooms; the walkway outside allows anyone to peer into any room that has its curtain open. Decor is economy motel style. The 1940s building is the resort's oldest.

• Eagle Ridge at Lutsen, $119–$309, is the only resort owned by the same family that owns Lutsen Mountains, and it's closest to the ski area. The pine exteriors of the buildings are rustic, but each unit, from studio to three-bedroom, has a fireplace, and many have whirlpools, in which guests can sit and watch the sun setting over Moose Mountain. Decor is basic upscale: track lighting, pale wood, textured carpets. There are indoor and outdoor pools, a sauna and a fitness center.

• The Mountain Inn at Lutsen, $99–$109, tucked into the forest just down the road. Decor is blandly attractive, and amenities are squeezed in: microwaves and fridges in some rooms, small hot tub, small sauna, small lobby in which to eat the complimentary breakfast of Danishes and coffee.

• Village Inn and Resort at Lutsen, across from the Mountain Inn and next to Eagle Ridge, is the biggest resort, with 111 units to rent, lodge rooms along with privately owned condos and townhomes. The big, attractive lobby has a stone fireplace and a cathedral ceiling, though it doesn't rival Lutsen lodge's intimacy. Lodge rooms, $115–$125, have dashes of character—stenciled bookshelves, small bay windows—and condos, $160– $250, are perfectly nice; however, the smallest, which sleep four, might spur claustrophobia in their tenants after more than a day. Townhomes rent for $300–$360, and executive lodges, which sleep 12, $550. The resort has two places to eat, one with an inviting saloon with fireplace. It has indoor and outdoor pools, a small playground, a skating pond, a stable offering sleigh rides and a supervised activities room for children 4 and up.

Many more rooms are available in Tofte, eight miles south of Lutsen:

• The 51-room Holiday Inn Express, $89, one suite at $229, right on Highway 61, doesn't have a view. It does have a vaulted pool room and a large and attractive lobby, with a wood-burning stone fireplace and many chairs and sofas where guests eat a large continental breakfast.

• Bluefin Bay, on the other side of the highway next to Lake Superior, has units that rent for $105–$139. Large units, $375, sleep eight and can be rented in three parts, $89, $179 and $195; each has two whirlpools and two fireplaces. Bluefin Bay's biggest assets are lake views, from its rooms and also from a large outdoor hot tub that is shielded from wind by a glass wall, an outdoor pool and a sauna.

❂ TRIP TIPS: Lutsen

• **Accommodations:**
Lutsen Resort, (800) 258-8736; Eagle Ridge, (800) 360-7666; Mountain Inn, (800) 686-4669; Village Inn, (800) 642-6036; Holiday Inn Express, (800) HOLIDAY or (218) 663-7899; Bluefin Bay, (800) 258-3346.
• **Lutsen Mountains,** (218) 663-7281.
• Lodge-to-lodge hiking along the Superior Hiking Trail and lodge-to-lodge skiing along the shore and the Gunflint Trail, (800) 322-8327.
• **Superior National Golf Course:** (218) 663-7195.
• **Snow conditions:** (800) 897-7669.
• **Information:** Lutsen-Tofte Tourism Association, (218) 663-7804.

Grand Marais
A Riviera for the rugged

The approach to Grand Marais was as spectacular as always. From the hairpin turn just north of the Cascade River, where an extra-wide shoulder serves as a balcony, we watched a wall of fog from Lake Superior advancing on the shoreline. Points of land, distinct and green, became dark gray, then a series of vague lumps, then a mere graininess within the fog bank. Elapsed time: two minutes.

This is a Riviera for the rugged, a remote section of the North Shore for those who bask in the lake's chill and revel in its unpredictability. Voyageurs, fur traders and Ojibwe first frequented Grand Marais' natural harbor, followed by trappers, prospectors, loggers and then the fishermen and small-business people who made it into a village. Tourists came, as did artists. Fishing waned as a livelihood but tourism increased, with hikers, skiers and canoeists heading for the Gunflint Trail.

I first visited Grand Marais in 1981, and my husband and I traveled there often until we had toddlers who couldn't be trusted on the rocky shores in front of our rented cabins. But then we returned, curious about reports that luxury vacation homes, franchises and tourist hordes had changed Grand Marais' character.

Instead, I was surprised at how little downtown Grand Marais has changed. Same Sven and Ole's pizza joint, packed each night. Same Beaver House bait-and-tackle shop, now with a walleye slicing through its roof and exhaling radio music from its toothy mouth. Same Lake Superior Trading Post, with $58 sweatshirts and 59-cent Genuine Hand-picked Rocky Mountain Huckleberry Bon-Bons. Same great Ben Franklin store, selling everything from Canadian toffee to wool socks and rabbit-fur hats.

The soda fountain, the bookshop, the World's Best doughnut shop—still flourishing. And the supposed takeover by franchises? A new Subway was on the highway on the town's outskirts, next to an auto-parts store and a coin-operated laundry. It didn't seem like such a blot on its landscape. The cute little twinkle lights over the art-jewelry shop seemed more out of place.

Mary MacDonald, administrator of the Grand Marais Playhouse, summarizes the local discussion as "quaintness vs. regular small town," with most people united against massive development. Whatever the perspective, nervousness isn't hard to understand. Grand Marais' character is worth preserving.

Everybody goes to Artist's Point, a rocky outcropping that reaches past the Coast Guard station into Lake Superior, and to the old lighthouse at the end of the harbor breakwall. To one side is the vast expanse of Lake Superior; to the other, bobbing sailboats, the village and the hazy outline of the Sawtooth Mountains.

As I pick my way toward the lighthouse, a line of young firefighters, fresh from duty in the Boundary Waters, marches by. In their yellow jackets and bandanas, with voyageur-like swagger, they are as picturesque as the harbor, whose beauty has inspired many painters. Swedish immigrant Anna Johnson, who came to Grand Marais in 1907, was the first artist to sell her work, and the Johnson Heritage Post showcases her work and those of other local artists.

At the Cook County Historical Museum, I learn about Birney Quick, the Minneapolis College of Art and Design professor who, in 1947, founded the Grand Marais Art Colony, which carries on his summer art classes. At the Sivertson Gallery, I buy "The Illustrated Voyageur" by local painter Howard Sivertson, who grew up in an Isle Royale fishing family in the 1930s and '40s and knows both the romance and menace of Lake Superior. We swim at the municipal pool, which also has a sauna, and I walk along Sweethearts Bluff Nature Trail from the adjoining campground.

Then we do what we always do: hike. Two of our favorite trails are near Grand Marais. Along the Kadunce River, the air is so crisp it tingles in our nostrils. We make a beeline for what my husband calls "God's perfect little place," a roomlike spot where the walls of the gorge come together and the rust-tinted water roars around a sitting ledge to make a waterfall.

Our trail, we notice, now is marked as access to the Superior Hiking Trail. South of Grand Marais, we arrive at the Upper Cascade, which we see now is part of the Superior Hiking Trail. My husband is scandalized. "How can they take my unknown hikes and put signs on them?" he wails. But the trail is even more lovely than we had remembered, lined with old cedars and feathery ferns. We come to an open spot at the bottom of a sheer rock escarpment, where we can clamber among boulders and watch the river tumble furiously around a bend in a series of small falls.

So what if the whole world knows about the beautiful spots around Grand Marais. There are enough of them to go around.

○ TRIP TIPS: Grand Marais

- **Events:** Second weekend in July, Arts Festival.
  First full weekend in August, Fisherman's Picnic, the North Shore's biggest festival.
- **Grand Marais Playhouse** puts on plays and schedules concerts, (218) 387-1648.
- **Grand Marais Art Colony:** For a schedule of workshops, call (218) 387-2737.
- **Accommodations:** East Bay Hotel downtown, 39 rooms. Rooms vary from an old-fashioned single with shared bath, $22, to a two-bedroom luxury suite, $125. (800) 414-2807.
  Grand Marais Recreation Area Campground, on the lakeshore and next to the municipal pool, $13–$17.50. (218) 387-1712.
  Naniboujou Lodge, 14 miles north, is a striking lakeshore lodge built in 1929. From mid-May to late October, its attractive rooms are $65–$85. The high ceiling of its dining room, which serves very good food, is painted with bright, geometric Cree designs; there's an adjacent solarium. Two-night winter weekends, including five meals, are $290–$350 for two. (218) 387-2688.
  Many other motels, B&Bs and cabins are in and around town.
- **Gunflint Trail:** From Grand Marais, this paved road stretches 63 miles through Superior National Forest and along the edges of the Boundary Waters Canoe Area Wilderness, dead-ending near the Canadian border. The trail is lined with resorts, where winter is as busy as summer: Snow falls early and stays late, so this is a mecca for cross-country skiers and dog-sled mushers. The 25 kilometers of the Pincushion Mountain trails begin just two miles from Grand Marais, and there are 200 kilometers

more farther along the trail. For information, call Pincushion B&B, (800) 542-1226; Bearskin Lodge, (800) 338-4170; Golden Eagle Lodge, (800) 346-2203; Boundary Country Trekking, (800) 322-8327; Gunflint Lodge, (800) 328-3325; Gunflint Pines, (800) 533-5814; or Borderland Lodge, (800) 451-1667.

• **Grand Portage:** Thirty-six miles north, costumed interpreters re-create the days of the fur trade at Grand Portage National Monument, a rebuilt stockade on the site of a famous fur post. A rendezvous and Ojibwe powwow are held the second weekend of August. (218) 387-2788.

• **Information:** Visitor Information Center, (800) 622-4014, (218) 387-2524.

2 MINNESOTA LAKE COUNTRY

Ely

Gateway to the Boundary
Waters Canoe Area Wilderness

Up through the Iron Range we drove, past a string of work-
ing-class towns, their mines still yielding taconite, until we
reached a town that once was one of them: Canoe World.

That's how I think of Ely, gateway to the Boundary Waters
Canoe Area Wilderness. It still sits on iron ore, but its streets today
are criss-crossed by ruddy people in Polarfleece, not miners.

It was the end of canoeing season, and outfitters' signs all
along Sheridan Street advertised "Used Equipment for Sale."
Side yards were stacked with canoes, and between them were
other northwoods businesses: stores selling moosehide muk-
luks and recycled-plastic anoraks, both linked to famous Arc-
tic explorers who live around Ely, and the antiques stores and
gift shops that follow tourists everywhere.

We drove through town and onto the Echo Trail, following
the eastern shore of pristine Burntside Lake. A cloud of snow
buntings scattered in front of us, and we turned down a gravel
road to Camp du Nord, a YMCA camp on the lake's North Arm.

A stag bounded across the road, zigzagging in front of our car.
Overhead, three adult bald eagles and a juvenile circled lazily.
Darkness fell, and above us a million points of light glowed. No
city skies, these; we gazed until our necks grew stiff.

It's what lies beyond Ely that has made it the favorite northwoods town of so many people, most notably former CBS
correspondent Charles Kuralt, who for years has trumpeted the
town's virtues and, in 1995, made good on his words by buying
WELY, its folksy, financially ailing radio station, and returning
it to the air.

Ely began drawing a new breed of tourist in 1978, when the
Boundary Waters was given its wilderness designation. Since
then, it has risen above the boom-and-bust economy of the
Iron Range and set its meter squarely on "boom."

On a hike along Bass Lake Trail, a loop six miles north of town, we struck up a conversation with a hiker who grew up in Ely.

"Things are changing so quickly," said Bryan Hoffmeister, who graduated from the high school in 1978 and now lives near the Twin Cities. "I liked Ely better when it was a mining, even a lumber town; now it's more touristy. But that's just my little selfish thing. Actually, it's much better that way."

About 15,000 of the people who go into the Boundary Waters each year enter through Ely. And the International Wolf Center, opened in 1993, brings another 50,000 a year.

The center is built around a handsome Science Museum of Minnesota exhibit that explores the symbolic power of the wolf on human folklore and the social dynamics among wolves, once exterminated in every state except Minnesota and Alaska.

But the biggest draw is the four resident wolves, "presented" twice a day. We showed up at the glass-walled viewing room early, and instantly one of the wolves burst out of the woods of their enclosure, snapping its teeth at a bevy of buntings. Its three siblings followed; they were born in 1993 in South Dakota.

Chris Hegenbarth, one of the naturalists, came to talk, mainly about what the wolves care about most: eating.

"A pack of four, typically in northern Minnesota, has a territory of 40 square miles," she said. "There might be 800 deer, and each wolf will get an average of 18 per year." She passed around the enormous foreleg of a moose.

"Notice that the hooves are bigger than a wolf's skull," she said. "Only 4 percent of the time do wolves get a moose."

Down the road, we visited another museum, sitting in a grove of red pine.

Its two cabins were dragged by dog sled from Knife Lake, near the Canadian border, after the 1986 death of Boundary Waters legend Dorothy Molter.

Molter, who first came to Ely in 1930, was the last person allowed to live within the BWCA, supporting herself by brewing root beer, which she gave to passing canoeists for donations. Today, the bottles she used and reused are collectors' items.

After watching a videotaped Molter discuss her simple lifestyle, it was time for a decision: tandoori chicken at the Minglewood Cafe, or grilled salmon with black-bean chile pesto at the

Chocolate Moose? After dinner at the Moose, an Ely gathering place, we walked through photographer Jim Brandenburg's overhead gallery, filled with gorgeous portraits of animals in the wild. Ely has a municipal sauna, but Camp du Nord has one, too, built in 1933 by the three local schoolteachers who began the rustic resort from scratch. That night, after a long parboil in the 170-degree heat, I plunged into the glacial lake and then sat outside with a woman who had just moved back to Minnesota after many years in California—"purgatory," as she called it.

"I like everything about this place," she said, gazing across the utterly quiet lake. "I could definitely live here."

It's a refrain that Bob Cary, editor of the *Ely Echo* and avid outdoorsman, hears often.

"People walk into the newspaper office and say, 'You people don't know how good you've got it,'" Cary growls. "And we say, 'We know exactly how good we've got it, you bozo.'"

✪ TRIP TIPS: Ely

- **Accommodations:** Camp du Nord is a family camp in the summer and rents cabins in other seasons. Choose carefully; comfort levels in cabins vary widely and do not always correspond to price. Best buys are Jack's and Lynx Lodge. The St. Paul YMCA, (612) 645-2136, handles reservations.

   The Northern Inn, 202 W. Sheridan St., has four small but comfortable rooms that share two baths, $40 with breakfast and use of kitchen and sauna. (800) 774-7520.

   The Holiday Inn Sunspree Resort, one mile from downtown, has 61 rooms overlooking Shagawa Lake, $89–$149. (218) 365-6565 or (800) HOLIDAY.

   There are many resorts around Ely, plus budget motels and B&Bs; call the chamber.

- **Excursions:** Two dozen outfitters and many resorts offer canoeing, skiing and dog-sledding excursions into the BWCA; the best-known dog-sledding outfit is Paul Schurke's Wintergreen Lodge, (800) 584-9425 and (218) 365-6022. Call the chamber for brochures.

- **BWCA permits:** In the winter, visitors use self-issuing permit stations at entry points. For overnight use between May 1 and Sept. 30, call (218) 365-7681 or (218) 365-7600 for information and (800) 745-3399 to reserve, starting Feb. 1.

- **Events:** Blueberry Arts Festival, last full weekend in July.

Harvest Moon Festival, weekend after Labor Day.
Voyageur Winter Festival, first through second weekend of
February.

- **International Wolf Center:** Daily from May to mid-October, Friday–Sunday the rest of the year. (800) 359-9653.
- **Dorothy Molter Museum**: Open weekends in May and daily from Memorial Day through September. (218) 365-4451.
- **Vermilion Interpretive History Center:** On the campus of Vermilion Community College in Ely, the center has exhibits on Will Steger's and Paul Schurke's North Pole expedition in 1986 and Schurke's Siberian expedition in 1989. Open Memorial Day to Labor Day, (218) 365-3226.
- **Nearby attraction:** The Tower Soudan Underground Mine State Park, 20 miles west of Ely, gives a fascinating underground tour, daily from Memorial Day through September. (218) 753-2245.
- **Information:** Ely Chamber of Commerce, (800) 777-7281.

Walker
Home of the spectacularly ugly eelpout

On lazy summer days, Walker is a classic northwoods Minnesota town.

I've been going to a lake resort near there with my family for years. We ride our bikes into town on the 28-mile Heartland Trail, eat ice cream from the Village Square and buy muskmelons and corn on the cob from the stand near the Amoco. On sticky afternoons, we drive the kids in to the big water slide.

The pace is slow, serene—unless a Crazy Day Sale falls on a cloudy day, in which case the resorts empty and shoppers crowd into the town of 1,100 like sheep to salt.

I thought I knew Walker. But when I turned up there during the winter, I found a different town. Walker had gone wild.

At the center of this turnabout is the eelpout, a roughfish that pops out of the depths mostly in winter, when it spawns. It's famous for its revolting looks and behavior to match:

When a fisherman pulls one out of a hole in the ice, the pout is likely to wrap its mottled, eel-like tail around his arm. Often, the pout announces its slimy self even before that.

"The thing is, half the time they crawl up backward," says Ken Bresley, who owns the Tackle Box bait shop in town. "You've had a few drinks, and you've never seen that before. It causes you to take a lot more drinks."

Bresley is the one who first hit on something important: Eelpout were created to be the butt of jokes. Jokes flow best on a tide of beer. Beer is what you drink when you're ice-fishing, and ice-fishing is what Walker's economy needed more of in the winter.

It was the beginning of a beautiful relationship.

Today, the International Eelpout Festival, which Bresley founded in 1979, brings more than 10,000 people to Walker every year for a rousing good time.

When I arrived in Walker on a sunny, warm Eelpout Saturday, I was amazed by the number of cars crawling through the streets, but that was nothing compared to the traffic on and around Leech Lake. As I walked through the grounds of Chase on the Lake, a Tudor-style hotel, a trio of snowmobilers roared up and circled me, looking as if they'd like to toss out a lasso. It put me on notice: The wide-open spaces of Leech Lake, Minnesota's third-largest, turn snowmobilers into ice cowboys, and unwary pedestrians into little dogies on a cattle drive.

I thought everyone not moving at 40 mph would be fishing, but that wasn't exactly true. Out on the ice, around an encampment dubbed Jurassic Pout, two women with deep tans were sitting on a sofa, playing cribbage. A string of pout lay abandoned on the ice, apparently the limit of the team's aspirations, and a man walked up with careful steps and urged me to take one home. A steadier Jurassic Pouter named Sherrie followed him. "We're just drinking today," she said.

Nearby, members of Club Oasis danced under plastic palm trees to an overamplified reggae tune with the refrain "We're Going on a Beer Run." Across a snowbank studded with pink flamingos, a pitcher was tossing iceballs, each of which coated the batter in a hail of slivers.

I looked inside the tent of Team Iowa, thinking I might find some fish being caught, but Team Iowa was sitting placidly around some Diet Cokes and Cheez Balls.

"We hit it pretty hard yesterday," explained Steve Kannegieter, who had driven up with his buddies from the northwest town of Sibley.

"We've been here two years now, and we haven't caught an eelpout yet," he said. "We can't keep those pesky walleye off our hook." He demonstrated an orange-and-white gadget called a Polar Tip-Up placed over the ice hole. "Actually, I've never caught anything with it," he added with a shrug. "We just like to drink and talk smart."

At the weigh-in station, I eyeballed an eelpout up close. The winner, an apparently gluttonous pout of nearly 13 pounds, was lying under the weighing table, its squashed face and bulging white belly turned toward me.

"That's a pig, not an eelpout," sneered the woman handing out souvenir copies of the *Pout-Independent,* a local newspaper known as the *Pilot-Independent* on other days.

A man in a white chef's toque bustled up and snatched a 7½-pound pout on the scale, the previous occupant of the display tub in the food tent having passed away. I followed him and joined the long line waiting for a $5 plate of fries and hot nuggets of fresh pout, which were delicious. As it turns out, no one badmouths the taste of the ugly pout, which is the only freshwater member of the cod family.

Then Ken Bresley walked by and urged me to go see the two-story ice house at the far end of the lake, which had, he said, an aquarium and a sauna. I wondered at the wisdom of the latter.

"This is the Eelpout Festival, it's not supposed to make sense," he said, then threw out his arms. "Look around you."

With that in mind, I got into my big, heavy car and drove onto the lake, the slush making slurping noises around my tires. I felt ridiculous using my turn signal in the middle of a lake, but I hadn't been in traffic that heavy since the State Fair.

The Pout Palace did have a sauna, standing in a half-foot of water, and it had a pout pen sunk into the ice under the snack table. There was a working fireplace built into one wall, and in another, two beer taps. Lots of ice holes had been drilled through the carpet, but no one was fishing. There wasn't enough room; people were packed together like strings of freshly caught pout, and filling themselves to the gills.

I'll see Walker differently when I visit next. For now I know that under that staid facade beats a very merry heart.

✪ TRIP TIPS: Walker

- **Events:** Moondance Jam, the weekend after July 4.
  Muskie/Northern Derby Days, end of July.
  Leech Lake Regatta, third weekend in August.
  Ethnic Fest, second weekend in September.
  North Country Marathon, third weekend in September.
  Eelpout Festival, the closing weekend of walleye season, around the third weekend in February.
- **Accommodations:** There are loads of resorts, plus motels and two B&Bs, Peacecliff, $62–$95, (218) 547-2832, and Tianna Farms, $45–$125, (218) 547-1306. Call for a guide.
- **Information:** Leech Lake Area Chamber of Commerce, (800) 833-1118.

Itasca

To Minnesotans, a hallowed spot

There were lace doilies on the polished oak table. In the bathroom, gold-tone faucets on the gleaming white pedestal sink. On the windows, heavy puffed curtains.

And on the bed frame, there was a small metal plate reading "Property of the State of Minnesota."

This is Douglas Lodge, part of the only summer resort run by the state. Once known as "a jewel standing in mud," it's served lodgers since 1905, when they came on foot or horseback. It's still a jewel; in 1994, renovations were completed that have given the old log lodge a level of luxury that seems unlikely in a state facility.

There's a reason for this: Minnesota has a soft spot for the park in which Douglas Lodge sits. Itasca State Park is the source of the Mississippi, home of 250-year-old pines as regal as California's redwoods and the inspiration for Minnesota's state-park system, which was one of the earliest in the nation and began with Itasca.

In a state full of beautiful parks, Itasca is special.

On the first day of the season, there was an air of excitement in Douglas Lodge. When my family and I walked down to the lobby after seeing our two-room suite, Joan the front-desk clerk was beaming.

"How do you like it?" she asked, knowing it was lovely. We didn't tell her we'd expected that, at $65, we'd probably have to bring our own sheets.

Outside, the park lay at our feet: Lake Itasca, stretching from Douglas Lodge to the Mississippi headwaters. Seventeen miles of paved biking trails. Twenty-four hiking trails. A pioneer cemetery and a grove of towering red pines named for the preachers who once convened there. Ancient burial mounds. A natural-history museum with a small amphitheater where naturalists put on daily programs in summer.

The first thing we did was run down to the lake, where red-winged blackbirds were everywhere, swaying from the tops of cattails. On the fishing dock, a boy was hauling in a perch. After that, we went over the list of 34 visitor favorites in the summer guide, checking off things we didn't want to miss, such as the self-guided nature trail and Old Timer's Cabin, built in 1934 by the Civilian Conservation Corps. The last time we'd visited Itasca, we'd rented bikes and ridden to the headwaters and back—typical day visitors, probably.

This time, we were more ambitious. We brought our own bikes and discovered a part of the trail we'd skipped before, the quiet, rolling stretch through the forest between Douglas Lodge and the rental shack. We were going to take the narrated boat tour of Lake Itasca, but got sidetracked at the beach.

During our stay, we picked up the story of the park. From the 17th century, explorers had tried to find the source of the great river. It finally was traced to Lake Itasca in 1832 by Henry Schoolcraft, led by an Ojibwe guide named Ozawindib, and named for the Latin verITAS CAput, for "true head." The area was settled slowly, until its dense pine forests attracted the attention of the lumber barons. In 1891, a far-sighted surveyor, Jacob Brower, got the Legislature to make Itasca Minnesota's first state park, but logging in the area didn't stop completely until 1919.

Even so, Itasca today holds the largest stand of 250-year-old pines left in Minnesota, though it's not very big. Visit the hushed Preachers Grove and try to imagine how the state looked before loggers stripped it of these majestic trees.

We didn't miss the evening program; we sat around a fire and listened as naturalist Dan Bera, in fringed buckskin, told us about the first campers in Itasca, 8,000 years ago, and how they hunted giant bison and made spears and arrowheads.

There's always something timely for Itasca's naturalists to talk about. In the late spring, showy lady's slippers bloom, and young animals can be sighted—fawns, fox, bear cubs. In July, young eagles and osprey are starting to fly about, and in August, loons grow more active. In September, especially around the second weekend, Bera says, the fall color is "just fantastic."

By the time we left, we'd knocked off 20 of the 34 "visitor favorites" but made hardly a dent in the trails. Of course, we'll go back.

Many people are regulars, and Bera begins to recognize their faces. Sometimes, he says, he asks why they keep coming back: "They say, 'Well, Itasca is *our* park.'"

☻ TRIP TIPS: Itasca

- **Accommodations:** The three suites in Douglas Lodge have private baths, a double bed and two single beds; $65. Four rooms share two baths; $40 double. Double rooms at Nicollet Court Motel, next to Douglas Lodge, go for $44. Cabins, some with kitchens, are $58 to $115. The Club House, a 1910 log building with 10 bedrooms, rents for $290. Reserve rooms and campsites as early as possible by calling the Connection, 922-9000 or (800) 246-2267. Lodgings and food service operate from Memorial Day weekend through the first weekend in October.

  The handsome Mississippi Headwaters Hostel, near the park headquarters, is open all year, making it a good place from which to ski Itasca's cross-country trails in winter. Six carpeted rooms hold four to eight bunk beds each; guests share three bathrooms and have access to a kitchen and a living room with stone fireplace. For members of Hostelling International, the nightly fee is $13, $9 for children. Nonmembers pay $16 and $11. For details or to reserve, contact the hostel at HC 05 Box 5A, Lake Itasca, Minn. 56560; (218) 266-3415.

- **Dining:** The dining room at Douglas Lodge serves food that can be good, but eating three meals a day there would be expensive. The Brower Inn, near the beach, serves snack food, such as pizza, hot dogs and popcorn.

- **Information:** (218) 266-2114.

Maplelag
A ski resort with personality

One winter, just as I was getting tired of cross-country skiing in the park reserve near my house, a yellow-and-brown newsletter fell into my lap.

It was from Maplelag, a cross-country ski resort north of Detroit Lakes. The newsletter was kind of quirky, packed with items about antique-lunchbox collections and talent shows and ski trails with names like Wavy Gravy.

It looked fun, and we signed up for a weekend. When we got to the resort, wood smoke was wafting through the air and a light snow was falling. In the lodge, we were met by Jim Richards, who owns and runs the place with his wife, Mary. As he showed us around the place, a woman overheard him and said to us, with a little smile, "It's the best place in the world."

The lodge was a scavenger's dream, the scavenger being Jim. On virtually every surface were old metal signs from railroad depots, Mexican diners and drugstores, plus a set of original Burma-Shave signs. Hopalong Cassidy and Dr. Seuss lunchboxes filled an entire wall, and 220 panes of stained glass were scattered among the buildings.

At 6:30 P.M., the dining room filled, and the weekend began. Mary Richards made a few announcements, and everyone sat down to spaghetti, salad and fry bread. Then, after a little ping-pong, my husband and I went outside to the hot tub.

A group of women from Winnipeg, red as boiled lobsters, had just gotten out. I sank in and let the snow melt on my shoulders as I gazed up at the bright flakes flying around gusts of steam. Pretty soon, we were so hot we had to get out and let the 10-degree air cool us down.

After that, the night seemed balmy.

Our room, built like a Pullman car, had a drawback: no bathroom. The last time I'd had to run outdoors to use a toilet had been Girl Scout camp, and I wasn't wild about it then. But we were newcomers; the regulars had booked up the cabins and rooms with bathroom access.

The next morning, we left our kids with high-school baby sitters and headed out. It was perfect ski weather: windless and bright, with fresh snow. The rolling, crisply groomed Twin Lakes trail passed stands of cattails and small lakes; when we paused, we could hear a woodpecker tapping in the otherwise silent woods. We skied for two exhilarating hours, occasionally passing others, but usually alone.

After lunch, I met Andy, a ski teacher from Norway, for a lesson. I and the other student, a chemistry professor from Michigan, wanted to practice turns, so Andy took us to Suicide Hill, where skiers were clustered like buzzards watching people crash. My husband was down at the sauna taking pictures of a Fargo man leaping into the frozen lake, so the man could brag to the folks back home. Our daughter was having her own lesson, slogging along patiently.

After dinner, I rewarded her with a session in the hot tub, this time under a sky filled with stars. As she bounced around, I talked with a Twin Cities man who has been visiting Maplelag since the early 1980s, when the Richardses ran it as a maple-syrup farm.

Then we heard clapping break out in the lodge; the talent show had begun. After the skits and recitals, a disc jockey showed up with funny balloons and Reese's Pieces, and pretty soon everyone was dancing polkas and making conga lines.

On Sunday morning, smorgasbord was served—smoked whitefish, herring, lefse, salami, crispbread and the biggest block of gjetost I've ever seen, plus eggs and fruit for the non-Nordic. Then I was out the door into bright sun. But Suicide Hill came back to haunt me. All my newly learned techniques deserted me as I concentrated on simply getting my sore muscles to move me forward. Eventually, my limbs loosened up, and I glided along past banks of sparkling snow.

Now we go to Maplelag every February, and we've graduated to a room with a bathroom just a few feet down the hall, which we appreciate—though I've never heard any other guest whisper a single word about bathrooms. At Maplelag, there's just too much else going on.

✪ TRIP TIPS: Cross-country resorts

- **Maplelag,** Route 1, Box 52, Callaway, Minn. 56521, (218) 375-4466 or (800) 654-7711. Maplelag ("lag" means community in Norwegian and is pronounced "log") has 53 kilometers of beautifully groomed trails. Rates for a weekend, including two nights and six meals and unlimited cookies and fruit, are $164 for adults, $124 for kids 8–14 and $98 for kids 4–7; families get a 10 percent discount. The same package midweek costs $120. The resort also is open in spring and fall; in the summer, it's part of the Concordia Language Villages network.

Another family resort, in north-central Wisconsin, is Palmquist's The Farm, N5136 River Road, Brantwood, Wis. 54513, (800) 519-2558 and (715) 564-2558. Like Maplelag, accommodations are in various buildings, but all have access to baths. The Farm has 28 kilometers of trails. A weekend package with five meals is $130 for adults, $65 for ages 5–11 and $52 for ages 3–4.

- For information on cross-country skiing trails, call Minnesota Tourism, (612) 296-5029 or (800) 657-3700, and Wisconsin Tourism, (800) 432-8747.

Spicer

Pyramids and a castle

Allen Latham was halfway through his lecture about Spicer and its history when he paused and looked slyly at those who had traveled to his inn on the shores of Green Lake.

"This time of year, cars only want to go north," he noted. "You probably had to fight with yours, right?"

Technically, we all had come north, according to the compass. But we knew what he meant: the Spicer—New London area in west-central Minnesota, though it includes a dozen lakes and a forested state park, isn't what most city folks consider north enough.

Railroad baron James J. Hill knew better. With John Spicer, town founder and Latham's grandfather, he put in rail links to Midwest cities in the 1880s; Spicer shipped out grain, and Hill shipped in tourists. The tourist boom peaked around 1900, Latham says, then faded. By the time World War II was over, the shores of Green Lake had become residential.

That's why, at first glance, the town of Spicer seems half-missing. There's a water slide, a lakefront restaurant, a cafe, a pub, a playground, a bed-and-breakfast—but no houses. Virtually everyone lives along Green Lake, four miles long between the generous beach of County Park 4, in Spicer's "downtown," and County Park 5 on its other side.

Once we figured this out, my daughter and I headed north along the lake, looking for the ancestral home Latham runs as an inn. On the way, we saw so many palatial houses, many of them new, that when we got to it, the 1893 Spicer Castle seemed rather homely.

As we walked up, a horse whinnied loudly from a wooded enclosure, and the fragrance of century-old white lilacs perfumed the air. The house was built as a traditional Queen Anne but became Tudor in 1913, after Spicer's daughter Jessie returned from Europe and had it remodeled, turning its peaked tower into a crenelated turret. Not much has changed since then, said Latham during a rambling teatime talk.

"There were two daughters who liked it the way it was and just left the place," he said. "The reason it's a B&B is to let people have fun with it a while longer without changing it."

We had a lovely tea—homemade coffeecake, delicate lemon butter drops and four other kinds of cookie, eaten on china with coffee poured from silver pots. But while everyone else got in the mood for a murder mystery set in 1930s England—Latham keeps things rolling as a Scotland Yard inspector—my daughter and I set off for a park in New London, just up the road.

There, the Little Crow Water Ski Club, most of them teenagers, were getting ready for their first weekly ski show of the season. The national water-ski show champions had been in the water for only two weeks, warned the announcer. There would be some "rough corners." Four of the jumpers had left for jobs at theme parks in Florida.

That said, the brightly costumed skiers hit the water and wowed us. We sat in the sand with 750 people on bleachers behind and watched as a 16-member ballet line, a four-tier pyramid, barefoot trick skiers and other acts sailed past. The evening was balmy, the music was loud, and we ate Snickers bars to the roar of marine engines—it was great, like being a teen-ager again. "I want to be in a ski show when I get older, I do, mom," my 6-year-old pleaded.

On the way back, we stopped at Little Melvin's, a handsome restaurant with an outside grill and patio tables, and looked out at Green Lake as we ate a fresh stone-crab sandwich and a sundae. At Spicer Castle, the murder mystery was in full swing; amid peals of laughter, we heard the suspects accuse each other of various nefarious deeds, including murder by hypnotic suggestion.

We slept in a high bed across from the portrait and rapier of Mason Spicer, a captain in the Spanish-American War, and awoke to an enormous breakfast of fruit, muffins, sausage and waffles with strawberries and cream.

There was one more thing to do. Borrowing a canoe, I took my daughter for a ride on the lake, the only place where she could see why local fishermen dubbed the house "Spicer's castle."

"It *is* a castle!" she cried, gratified.

☢ TRIP TIPS: Spicer and New London

- **Events:** The Little Crow Ski Club puts on ski shows every Friday evening in New London's Neer Park, June through Labor Day, and at special events. There's no charge, but donations are requested.

- **Recreation:** The Glacial Lakes Trail is paved along the 12 miles between Willmar and New London, and another six miles of compacted granite continues to Hawick. Sibley State Park is four miles west of New London and has a beach, trails, campsites and daily nature programs in summer. Call (320) 354-2055.

- **Accommodations:** Spicer Castle has 10 rooms, $60–$115, with private but cramped baths. Of two cabins, the most popular is John's Cottage, with fireplace and whirlpool, $130. Murder mysteries with a five-course dinner are scheduled almost every weekend; participants needn't be guests. Call (800) 821-6675 or (320) 796-5870.

  Indian Beach Resort on Green Lake is a tidy family resort with a harbor, lodge and 23 cottages, which rent for $450–$1,150 per week during summer. Call (320) 796-5616.

  Green Lake Inn is a B&B in Spicer's downtown. Four richly decorated rooms, two with bay windows overlooking the lake, cost $69–$89. Call (320) 796-6523.

  County Park No. 5 is a pleasant, full-service park on Green Lake with a store, boat rental and 45 campsites, $11. Call (320) 796-5564.

- **Restaurants:** Melvin's on the Lake in Spicer, (320) 796-2195.
- **Information:** Willmar Chamber of Commerce, (320) 235-0300.

3 MISSISSIPPI RIVER TOWNS

Red Wing
A frontier boom town that lasted

From the day the first eager entrepreneur stepped off the dock, Red Wing has been the little town that could.

Like other frontier boom towns, it rode the waves of prosperity; its trick, however, was always bouncing back after the hard knocks.

Partly, it's due to a charmed location: For centuries before the white settlers came, there was a thriving village within this sharp elbow of the Mississippi River, in the shadow of Barn Bluff. For the 300 Santee Dakota who lived there in bark houses, it was a nice place: scenic, fertile, on a water highway.

Of course, this also made it attractive to white settlers, who eventually took it for themselves and named it for the local Dakota chiefs, descended from an ancestor who carried a swan's wing dyed scarlet.

The fertile fields and river made the new town, for a time, the largest primary grain market in the world. But when the wheat centers moved west, other industries developed—among them, leather and, from the abundant local clay deposits, pottery.

Today, those industries have made a name for Red Wing that goes far beyond regional boundaries. Starting in 1877, the crocks and jugs of Red Wing Stoneware became fixtures in town and rural kitchens. The plant closed in 1967, but the grandson of the last president continues as co-owner of Red Wing Pottery Sales, which carries 500 patterns of dinnerware.

"A lot of people drive a long way to see us," says Scott Gillmer. "For a long time, we were the only tourist attraction."

In 1982, the big brick factory next door reopened as Pottery Place, an outlet and retail center, and in 1987, potter John Falconer bought the rights to the name Red Wing Stoneware and began making the familiar crocks with speckled blue Bristol glaze, so durable, he says, "you can take a nail and scratch the surface and see only a silver line from the metal."

And all along, collectors have kept Red Wing a pottery capital, swelling its population during the annual July convention and occasionally providing a bit of buying frenzy—4-inch butter churns that Red Wing Stoneware made and sold to an Iowa collectors club for $15, Falconer says, were being traded the day of issue for $130. "But that doesn't happen to every piece," he says modestly.

Red Wing Shoes also has spread the red-wing logo throughout the world; its store in the renovated Riverfront Centre is one of 400. It's been growing since its founding in 1905, and its boots and shoes, still made with leather from a local tannery founded in 1873, now are sold in 80 countries.

Red Wing Shoes also was responsible for restoring the 1875 St. James Hotel, which it bought in 1977 and now is so popular that weekend reservations should be made up to six months in advance. It also helped rejuvenate the Sheldon Theatre, bequeathed to the city by one of its many tycoons in 1900 and reopened with its original glitter in 1988.

Today, visitors, especially from the big city, consider Red Wing small-town America at its best. Many come to shop at the stores in and around Pottery Place, in the St. James shopping court and downtown.

Three historic districts are thick with the handsome houses built by men who became rich on grain, lumber, banking and terra cotta; three of them are B&Bs, and one, the octagonal Lawther House, is an antiques store. The Sheldon, a stop on the vaudeville circuit in its early days, has concerts, theater or other performances nearly every weekend.

Amtrak passenger trains rumble through town several times a day, linking Red Wing with St. Paul, La Crosse and Chicago. In season, tugs push barges up and down past Levee Park and, beyond the still-busy Continental Grain elevator, past Bay Point Park.

"It's part of the mystique of Red Wing, that the tourism and industry seem to work together," says Allen Anderson, director of the visitors bureau. "For us, tourism is the frosting on the cake."

✪ TRIP TIPS: Red Wing

- **Accommodations:** For weekends, reserve early.
    St. James Hotel, $75–$155. Attractive rooms that come with champagne at night, hot drinks in morning. (612) 388-2846, (800) 252-1875.
    Candlelight Inn B&B, $85–$135, 1877 Victorian near downtown, four attractive bedrooms and a very nice suite, (612) 388-8034.
    Golden Lantern Inn B&B, $89–$125, 1934 Tudor Revival with five bedrooms and acres of lovely wood, (612) 388-3315.
    Pratt-Taber Inn B&B, $89–$110, 1876 Italianate a block from Sheldon. Six rooms, not all equal; try Polly's, with fireplace and bath. (612) 388-5945.
- **Events:** River City Days, first full weekend in August.
    Fall Festival of Arts, second weekend in October.
- **Sheldon Theatre:** Call (612) 388-2806 or (800) 899-5759 for a schedule of performances.
- **Tours:** 1 P.M. weekdays at Red Wing Stoneware, north of downtown off Highway 61. (612) 388-4610, (800) 352-4877.
    1 P.M. Saturdays at the Sheldon, plus Thursdays and Fridays in summer, including an 18-minute movie on Red Wing history, $2.50.
- **Bicycling:** The trailhead of the scenic, 20-mile Cannon Valley Trail is near Pottery Place, off Bench Street. (507) 263-3954.
- **Skiing:** Mount Frontenac, nine miles south; call 388-5826.
- **Museums:** The Goodhue County Historical Museum, (612) 388-6024, on the bluff in back of town, has a great view and also interesting exhibits. It's at 1166 Oak St. (turn up West Street, right onto Seventh Street, follow signs).
- **Information:** (612) 388-4719, (800) 762-9516.

Wabasha
A roost for the eagle-eyed

In Wabasha, the houses have eyes.
This small Mississippi River town is full of people who peep out windows at their neighbors and then set the phone lines buzzing. Except here, the neighbors are bald eagles, and the

watchers are locals who love to see them dive, swoop and chase each other.

"A lot of people in town have spotting scopes," says Mary Rivers, who coordinates the volunteers who staff the city's Eagle Watch Observatory and often receives phone calls that start out, "You've got to come see this!"

Each year, Wabasha residents have more to watch. Since DDT was banned in 1972, bald eagles have made a spectacular comeback. And not only is Wabasha right on the avian freeway to the south, but the area is the best place in the state to watch the birds in the winter: Just north of town, across from Reads Landing, the Chippewa River empties into the Mississippi, providing a reliably open patch of water to year-round eagles and migrating snowbirds from the north.

One January, a friend and I traveled to Wabasha to see if we could spot a few of what Rivers calls "avian jumbo jets." We drove down in the dark and checked into the Anderson House, where we immediately felt the truth of its claim to "a feeling of time having stopped." No Laura Ashley heirloom look here; just an indefinable aroma of age, the hissing of radiators and massive, dark furniture, much of it bought for the hotel's opening in 1856.

Later, after the hotel's inexpensive seafood buffet, we walked down the street to the silent downtown. Fat, glimmering flakes of snow were falling, and we had the eerie feeling of being on a movie set. Except for an occasional sighting of glum men hunched over beers behind the town's century-old storefronts, and the unseen presence of a baker frying doughnuts, whose aroma followed us everywhere, we were utterly alone.

An old Gambles store, a shabby grain elevator, an American Legion with red, white and blue doors—it could have been Bedford Falls of *It's a Wonderful Life*. Wabasha has indeed been the setting of a movie, *Grumpy Old Men*, although it was filmed elsewhere in Minnesota.

Back at the Anderson House, we picked out a cat for the night—the hotel has made a name for itself lending cats to guests—and sat on the patchwork quilt in our corner room, gazing out at the snow flying by in the light of old-fashioned street lamps, vaguely aware of the river somewhere nearby.

The next day, we saw it—right out our windows. Down the

street, we found the town's Eagle Watch Observatory, a large wood deck with exhibits and a carved statue of an eagle. We looked and looked: no eagles.

So we walked back up to Main Street and to Old City Hall Antiques, an engaging mix of stores, then drove six miles down Highway 61 to Kellogg and the Meadowlark Shops.

The anchor of the little complex overlooking the highway is L.A.R.K. Toys. Proprietor Donn Kreofsky greeted us and gave us a fast rundown on the place, directing our eyes to the big carved troll in the rafters above and mentioning the Christmas shop and the pet pot-bellied pig. But what really grabbed us was Kreofsky's basswood carousel. The more we gaped, the more we spotted—a dragon ridden by a wizened little wizard, a turtle with a seashell atop its own, a troll atop a pig. I had a hard time dragging my friend away. "This is really cool," she said, eyes glittering.

Finally, it was time to meet Mary Rivers at the Eagle Watch Observatory. "Look for the black blobs in the trees," she said, and we immediately spotted two across the river. It was a cold day, so they were "loafing"—conserving energy, waiting for the easiest catch.

Our toes began to feel numb, so we decided to adjourn to the Wabasha Boatworks a block north, a restaurant that has a big window overlooking the river. But, on Rivers' suggestion, we first drove a block south, toward some big cottonwoods. Bingo! An eagle flew overhead, and we stopped the car and jumped out to watch; you can do that in Wabasha.

At the Boatworks, over hot chocolate laced with Bailey's, we peered at two more eagles across the river—just loafing, though. So we listened to Rivers' stories: about the eagle who got its talons stuck in a fish so big it nearly drowned him, until it ate the fish off its feet; about four-eagle dogfights over fish; about the balmy day in mid-December when Rivers saw 300 of them at Reads Landing.

"I just stood there with my mouth open," she told us. "They were so gorgeous. You could see the fish wiggling in their talons, and sometimes they'd drop and hit a car on the highway."

We despaired of ever having nifty stories to tell. But, on the way home, at Reads Landing, we were rewarded. Two eagles in trees, and then, in quick succession, on long, slow glides, two overhead. It was enough.

☼ TRIP TIPS: Wabasha eagle-watching

- **Eagle-watching:** In November and December, depending on the weather, eagles migrate south, and from mid to late February through March, they fly back. On Sunday afternoons from November through March, observatory volunteers talk about eagles and let people look through spotting scopes.
- **Events:** Grumpy Old Men Festival, last Saturday in February.
      Dockings of the *American, Mississippi* and *Delta Queens,* with bands, "quite an event, like an old-time arrival," says the chamber's Jane McLagen, April–October.
      Riverboat Days, fourth full weekend in July.
      Volksmarch, second Saturday of October.
- **Accommodations:** Anderson House, (612) 565-4524 or (800) 862-9702, with rooms for $50–$125. Bridgewaters B&B around the corner has five rooms, $58–$145, (612) 565-4208; Eagles on the River B&B has views and a private beach, two rooms, $99–$149, (800) 684-6813, (612) 565-3509.
- **Information:** Call the Chamber of Commerce, (612) 565-4158.

Lake Pepin
Three villages along the bluffs

It's a beautiful spring Saturday. The sap is running, the birds are chirping, and the car is sitting in the driveway, just waiting to be taken for a drive.

Where do you go?

Join the crowd and head down Wisconsin 35 along the shores of Lake Pepin, the 30-mile-long widening of the Mississippi River.

It's a drive city folk in particular like: picture-postcard views, mainly, but also interesting little shops and galleries, superb dining and a romantic history that includes handsome French fur traders and lovelorn Indian maidens.

Therefore, Lake Pepin is not neglected. In the fall, when the trees along the bluffs burst into reds and yellows, a steady stream of traffic winds down the highway, weekend crowds trample through the antique stores and the wait for a table at the Harbor View Cafe in Pepin stretches to four hours.

In the winter, the shops and cafes go dormant. But when the air warms in mid-March, people start trickling back—and Lake Pepin is ready for them.

One year, I drove down on the second Saturday of March. The tawny limestone outcroppings above the river highway were gleaming, bathed in the first wan rays of spring; the ice on the lake was starting to darken as water flowed underneath.

In Stockholm, a steady stream of customers filed through Crocus Oak, studying its collection of rustic log chairs, picnic baskets, old license plates, an antique tricycle and jewelry, all 25 percent off. "It's kind of a season-opener sale," proprietor Laurence Schultz said jovially.

Tiny Stockholm, jammed into the shadow of a bluff, has a shop for every seven residents. Almost all have opened since the early '80s, when artisans and shopkeepers began moving into the old clapboard and limestone buildings.

At Amish Country, customers moved between $1,000 quilts and polished armoires, murmuring in reverent tones, as if in a museum. There was one bargain: a pile of beautiful miniature quilts—well, potholders—going for $7 for a pair.

Across the street, at Stockholm Antiques, Sharon Emery of Minneapolis was fingering a bowl of irresistibly smooth marble balls. Emery and her husband, Dick Gilyard, had just had lunch at the Harbor View Cafe in Pepin, which had opened the day before. How was it? "Wonderful," Emery said with a satisfied smile.

"When the Harbor View opens, that usually signals the start of the season," says Lucy Elliott, who runs Stockholm Antiques and the adjoining Merchants' Hotel, an 1864 limestone building in which she rents out three rooms.

In Pepin, a maroon van filled with restless people was parked outside the blue-and-white Harbor View, awaiting its 5 P.M. opening. Next door, goldsmith Rebecca Paquette-Johnson was sitting behind the counter of her Bnox Gold & Iron as the afternoon sun streamed through her tall windows. "There's something about the water and the Harbor View that brings them in," she said.

The name of her business, she said, is a longtime endearment used but never explained by her husband's grandmother and grandfather, who summered in Pepin. She pointed to an old photograph near the door, showing a handsome young man and woman in a canoe.

Her husband, Ted Johnson, came down the street and stood in the doorway just as a train thundered past across the street. "You get used to it," he shouted.

Seven miles away, high above the lake on rolling farmland, three cars were parked at the Little House Wayside, where author Laura Ingalls Wilder was born in 1867. None of the visitors were Japanese, though: "Little House" sites in Wisconsin and Minnesota are enormously popular among Japanese tourists.

To Japanese, the re-created log house must seem pretty exotic. Others may feel sadness at the sight of the cabin, plopped amid the silos and farmhouses that replaced Pa Ingalls' beloved Big Woods and sparked an exodus that saw the family moving to eight different places in 10 years.

Back in Stockholm, the day was waning. Three towheaded girls were playing skin the cat in the birch tree outside Stockholm Pottery and Mercantile. Nearby, in the Short Stop Cafe, Linda and Dennis O'Malley of St. Paul were sitting contentedly over cups of coffee, having spent the day poking around both sides of the lake and the previous night dining at the Harbor View.

That night, they would again be staying at the Harrisburg Inn B&B in Maiden Rock, which they liked. "It's like your mom and dad taking care of you," Linda O'Malley said.

At the Harrisburg Inn, Carol Crisp was stirring ingredients for the next morning's potato-broccoli egg bake. The inn, built on rock just above the highway, advertises itself as "A View With a Room," and the slogan is justified: All four of its rooms, two with balconies, have sweeping views of the lake and its often-spectacular sunsets.

In Maiden Rock, business was brisk at Ole's Bar, famous for its Ole burgers, but the Maiden Lane shops—used books, antiques, art—in an old, unheated creamery just off the highway, awaited warmer weather. Sea Wing Gifts was closed for the day, but taped to the door was a copy of *The Legend of Maiden Rock* by Margaret A. Persons, whose version of the story has the Dakota maiden Winona leaping off the "towering granite mass" with the still-warm body of her Chippewa lover as the assassins sent by her father close in.

Very romantic, in an overblown, European kind of way. As it happens, the rock in question is just outside Stockholm, not

Maiden Rock, which, in summer, is favored more by motorcy-
clists and campers than by poets.

Down at the Harbor View Cafe, the doors had opened, the
maroon van had disgorged its load, and waiters were taking orders for grilled Chilean sea bass, cassoulet with lamb and
sausage and fresh catfish with ginger-black bean sauce. Soon,
the waiting list would be started. The season along Lake Pepin
had begun.

✪ TRIP TIPS: Wisconsin's Lake Pepin

- **Dining:** The Harbor View Cafe in Pepin is open from mid-March
  to Thanksgiving; call (715) 442-3893 for exact times. Until April,
  it's open 11 A.M. to 2:30 P.M. and 5–9 P.M. Friday, 11 A.M. to 2:30
  p.m. and 4:45–9 P.M. Saturday and noon to 7:30 P.M. Sunday.
  Then Thursdays are added, and on Memorial Day, Mondays
  are added, with closing at 8 P.M.

  No reservations. Hosts take names and estimate waits, which
  are two to three hours on Saturday nights. Many people bring canoes, says co-owner Paul Hinderlie, and explore the Chippewa
  River bottoms while waiting. Others walk along the breakwater,
  and some bring bikes to ride on little county roads; staff will suggest routes.

  The Jenny Lind Cafe in Stockholm, (715) 442-2358, serves
  homemade baked goods, soups and salads and also is very popular. It's pleasant to drink coffee outside next to its perennial gardens.

- **Lodgings:** The Harrisburg Inn B&B in Maiden Rock, (715) 448-
  4500, has four rooms, $68–$88.

  Merchants' Hotel in Stockholm, (715) 442-2113, has three
  rooms with shared bath, $45–$55, and opens in mid-April.

  Members of the Wisconsin B&B Homes and Historic Inns Association include Pine Creek Lodge, $85, (715) 448-3203, and
  Hyggelig Hus, $85–$95, (715) 442-2086, in Stockholm; A Summer Place in Pepin, $65–$95, (715) 442-2132; and the Gallery
  House in Alma, $65–$85, (608) 685-4975.

- **Events:** Maiden Rock Summerfest, third Saturday in June.

  Stockholm Art Fair, third Saturday in July.

  Laura Ingalls Wilder Days in Pepin, third weekend in September.

- **Nightlife:** The Lake Pepin Players perform theater in summer.
  (800) 823-3577.

- **Museums:** In Pepin, the Depot Museum (trains), April through October, and Pepin Historical Museum (local history, including Laura Ingalls Wilder), mid-May through mid-October.
- **Information:** (715) 448-4500 (Maiden Rock), (715) 442-5162 (Stockholm), or (715) 442-3011 (Pepin).

Trempealeau
Happy trails for everyone

On the hotel lawn, people in Peruvian sweaters and jean jackets played hacky sack in a light drizzle. Reggae issued from outdoor speakers, and the aroma of jerk chicken drifted from food booths.

On the deck, waiting reggae fans watched the tugboat Lady Lone Star go by and suspended conversation for thundering freight trains. Trains could be spotted on the other side of the Mississippi, too, threading their way along the feet of misty green bluffs.

Across the street, two visitors examined a whimsical oasis that includes topiary monkeys and a miniature Japanese garden, complete with a bamboo bridge, mountains and pagoda, and chatted with the resident of the small house next to it. "See, it's just like Jamaica," one of the moist visitors said cheerfully. "You have a beautiful garden, and you live in a hut."

This is Trempealeau, Wisconsin, a struggling river town until a guy with a ponytail and his partner bought a dumpy old hotel in 1986, fixed it up and brought imported beer, vegetarian food and live blues to town. Two years later, the 24-mile Great River State Trail brought bicyclists, too.

Today, the Trempealeau Hotel has a loyal following—1,260 people showed up for the annual Reggae Sunsplash on a day when the rain never really stopped—that appreciates it for the small-town rarity it is. At the Trempealeau, the people are friendly, the food is fresh and the air is smoke-free.

There are few shops in Trempealeau, and there's not much to look at besides the Japanese garden and the stone ruins of the Melchior brewery, left over from an 1888 fire that wiped out all but five of the town's buildings.

Trempealeau is a place for doing, not looking. The Great River trail, which runs through two wildlife refuges, is one of Wisconsin's best for spotting birds and animals. Perrot State Park, on the outskirts of town, includes hiking and canoeing trails and spectacular views, including one, across a bay of the Trempealeau River, of a hill French explorers called La Montagne Qui Trempe a l'Eau, "the mountain that soaks in the water."

To the south of town is a marina and the Upper Mississippi River National Wildlife and Fish Refuge, where the 4½-mile Long Lake Canoe Trail traverses backwater sloughs and islands, an area Trempealeau Hotel founder Bill King calls "safariland, Wisconsin style." Fishing is good, and Lock and Dam No. 6 is an attraction for those who love to watch the rise and fall of barges through locks.

When my daughter and I were at the hotel, we were happy to simply sip drinks on the sunlit porch, gazing out at the river. After a dinner of walnut burgers with tomato and sprouts—the hotel has become famous for them—we took a stroll around town and then settled into the Fun Room, a big corner room with three windows, a single and double bed and attractive pine furniture.

The bathroom was shared, but because there were only a few other guests, we never had to wait to use it. The other seven rooms were very small, but most were cheerful and had beds furnished with bright quilts.

After breakfast, we headed for Perrot State Park, named for Nicholas Perrot, a French trader and diplomat who spent the winter of 1685–86 on the site. We first walked the Black Walnut Nature Trail, learning from frequent, detailed signs such things as how "eye holes" get into sandstone outcroppings. Then we climbed down to the Riverview Trail, from which we watched an egret walking delicately through the shallow bay water.

At the park's nature center, we struck up an acquaintance with Greg Menig, of Arlington Heights, Ill., who was working his way toward the Pacific Ocean on his bicycle.

But Trempealeau, he said, was an irresistible respite. He saw the posters for the reggae festival, set up camp in the park, made friends at the party, treated himself to two nights in the hotel and completely neglected his journal.

"It's been great," he said with a happy grin. "But tomorrow, it's time to go back to work."

❂ TRIP TIPS: Trempealeau

- **Accommodations:** From April through October, the Trempealeau Hotel rents a cottage on its grounds, $65, in addition to its rooms, $30–$35; call (608) 534-6898.

  Two motels offer traditional amenities: the River View, $38–$46 for two, (608) 534-7784; and Pleasant Knoll, $40–$60, (608) 534-6615.

  Perrot State Park has 104 campsites; call (608) 534-6409.

- **Events:** Spring Bike Tour, second Saturday in May.

  Reggae Sunsplash at the Trempealeau Hotel, third Saturday of May.

  Blues Bash at the Trempealeau Hotel, first Saturday after Memorial Day.

  Catfish Days, the weekend after the Fourth of July.

  Stars Under the Stars concerts; call (608) 534-6898 for a schedule.

- **Recreation:** Perrot State Park rents canoes. Tremplo Bike Shop, (608) 534-6217, rents bicycles.

  The Great River trail connects with the La Crosse River Trail, which connects with the Elroy-Sparta and 400 trails to provide 100 miles of crushed-limestone trails. From Wisconsin 35, the trailhead is reached via the Marshland access of the Trempealeau National Wildlife Refuge, 8½ miles north of town, though most people ride from town or Perrot State Park.

- **Information:** Trempealeau chamber, (608) 534-6780.

La Crosse
Idyllic cruises on an old steamboat

The cruise of the *Julia Belle Swain* to Winona was jinxed. First, the water was too high to dock in Winona, and the two-hour lunch stop there had to be scrapped. The night before departure, the captain ran into an errant skater and broke a front tooth. At departure, a huge barge had just started through the lock north of La Crosse, tying it up for two hours, so a new southward course had to be set. Then the chef cut his finger to the bone on a meat slicer.

Well, this isn't the *Tinker Belle* on the Never-Never River; it's a real steamboat, on the real Mississippi, with real weather and real people.

The best thing about the *Julia Belle* is that she goes real places—making regular stops in Winona and Prairie du Chien, along part of the Mississippi's most scenic stretch.

Robert Kalhagen, the Madison, Wisconsin, businessman who brought the *Julia Belle* to La Crosse in 1995, says he always has been fascinated with the role steamboats and rivers played in frontier history.

"We want to take people places to see things, rather than go around in circles," he says.

But even minus the stop in Winona, my trip on the *Julia Belle Swain* was idyllic.

As we pushed off from Riverside Park, sunlight began to seep through the sullen skies, brightening the boat's white-iron trim and the American flag whipping in the breeze. Morning mist clung to the tops of the conical green hills on the shore, and a heron flapped low over the gray water.

I stood on the third deck and listened to the boat: to the rhythmic exhalations of steam from the smokestack, to the shoosh-shoosh of the paddle wheel hitting water. The *Julia Belle* was built in 1971 around 1915 steam engines, taken from an old Louisiana ferry, and her machinery is something to see: massive red and white pistons on long yellow rods, slowly sliding into their steam cylinders with an oily wheeze and back out, through the rear of the first deck, then back again. "Logged more than a million miles," a sign proclaims.

Rice Krispie bars and party mix were set out in front of the big, hand-painted back bar on the second deck; two teen-age boys had grabbed a stash and headed to the more intimate third deck with a Scrabble board. There, a woman from Sparta, Wisconsin, was admiring the plush interior and intricately carved calliope. "Isn't this great?" she asked. "It's really something."

Overhead, in the glass pilothouse, captain Randy Morrison was gobbling Tylenol and waiting for his dentist to call back on the cellular phone. "This is a lovely part of the river," he said, his bruised jaw clenched. "Normally, we'd be making more announcements, about the scenery and river history."

River navigation today isn't as treacherous as it was in the 1800s, Morrison said, but wind and high water keep the job interesting. "It's long stretches of tedium broken by a few moments of sheer terror," he said.

I headed down to the sunny edge of the first deck and stretched out in a lounge chair with a good book. But pianist Scott Warner and vocalist Carolyn Nelson began a smooth set of jazz standards—"Summertime," "Take the A-Train," "World on a String"—so I settled at a table to listen and gaze out at the wisps of steam floating toward the Wisconsin bluffs.

At Genoa, the *Julia Belle* turned around, and the chef, despite his heavily bandaged hand, served ham sandwiches, potato salad and brownies. Warner and Nelson played more sets, I got in a wonderfully relaxing hour with my book, and soon La Crosse was in view. By then, the Saturday boating crowd was out in full force, and every neck was craned toward the big blue-and-white wedding cake on water.

As we landed, a man with two small boys ran up to the rail, excited. "Where did you come from?" he asked. "Did you come from St. Louis?" When I told him the boat's home was La Crosse, his face fell: "Oh," he said. "I thought it was something special."

Well, guess what: She is.

✪ TRIP TIPS: La Crosse and the *Julia Belle Swain*

Julia Belle Swain: From mid-May through October, two-day trips to Prairie du Chien and back, $229 per person double occupancy, $119 per child 12 and under in same room; one-day trips to Prairie du Chien with breakfast, lunch and dinner, $99 including the bus trip back; two-day trips to Winona, $199; one-day trips to Winona, $59, including bus trip back; five-hour cruise downriver, $39. For a schedule, call (800) 815-1005.

La Crosse:
- **Accommodations:** A Radisson, (608) 784-6680, is right across the street from Riverside Park, with rooms at $99–109, but there's a small, friendly hotel near Heileman Brewery, the Guest House Motel at 810 S. Fourth St., with $44 double rooms ($33 single), cable, free coffee and a small outdoor pool. Call (608) 784-8840. Also: the Martindale House B&B, an 1850s Italianate home with four rooms and a carriage house, $69–$145. (608) 782-4224.
- **Nightlife:** The Pump House Regional Arts Center, (608) 785-1434, programs concerts and plays from September to May, with special events in summer. It also compiles an arts and enter-

tainment guide, Revue, and has an after-hours information line, (608) 784-2787.

- **Brewery tours:** G. Heileman gives free tours daily June–August and Monday through Saturday September–May. (608) 782-2337, (800) 433-2337 outside Wisconsin.
- **Events:** Riverfest in Riverside Park, Fourth of July weekend.
    Log Boom and Rendezvous in Pettibone Park, first full weekend in August.
    Great River Jazz Fest on the Oktoberfest Grounds, first or second weekend in August.
    Great River Traditional Music and Crafts Festival, third or fourth weekend in August.
    Oktoberfest, first weekend in October.
- **Information:** La Crosse visitors bureau, (800) 658-9424.

Northeast Iowa
Hairpin turns and breathtaking panoramas

The road, part of an innocent-looking rural landscape, was familiar: a long, ear-popping swoop down. Then, a long, slow struggle up. A few miles later: another swoop, another struggle.

The first time I saw this road, I was on a weeklong bike trip. I'd pedaled into southwest Wisconsin, to an area known as Little Switzerland. Then I'd pedaled across the bridge at Prairie du Chien, thinking I'd follow the river south.

And wound up in Little Everest.

Yes, this is northeast Iowa, and it has killer hills. Its bluffs above the Mississippi are way, way up. If you want to get to a town, you have to go way, way down. Take the stomach-churning road to Clayton. At its bottom—you think—there's a big sign: "Trucker—You're Not Out of Danger Yet."

My first trip left me with an impression of pretty river towns and a striking landscape. But only an impression: On a bike, the view tends to be either a 40-mph blur or an excruciatingly slow march of concrete.

In a car, the panorama unfolds more gently.

When this area was being settled in the years before the Civil War, the river towns of northeast Iowa did a flourishing business in grain shipping. Fortunes were made; mansions were built. But in this century, their usefulness waned, and they became sleeping beauties, lying quietly in their river coulees.

For years, no one paid them much attention, but that's changed.

This stretch of the Mississippi, part of a 260-mile-long wildlife and fish refuge, is one of the most beautiful. It's breathtaking, if you're looking at it from the 450-foot-tall bluffs above Lansing, or from Pikes Peak near McGregor. From the banks, the procession of rounded, tree-covered hills makes it look much like the Rhine Valley; if this were Germany, some of the more distinctive ones might have romantic names: Siegfried's Throne, perhaps, or the Seven Sisters.

From the Minnesota border, the Great River Road snakes from one town to another, each hugging the river. In Lansing and McGregor, houseboats and pontoons can be rented for explorations of the islands and sloughs of the Upper Mississippi River Wildlife and Fish Refuge. Marquette is the home of a big gambling boat, the *Miss Marquette*. Guttenberg has a milelong city park along the river, with one end at Lock and Dam 10; if you like to watch really big barges, this is the place for a picnic.

The scenery starts in earnest at Lansing, 12 miles south of the Minnesota border and linked to Wisconsin by Blackhawk Bridge, named for the Sauk chief who resisted white settlement and whose band was massacred near here in 1832. The bustling little town is built on a hill. Climb to the top of that hill, via a few hairpin curves, and you're in Mount Hosmer City Park, which commands a spectacular, three-state view of the bridge, river valley and town.

A few miles down the road is Effigy Mounds National Monument, in which 191 ancient burial mounds, 29 in the likeness of bears and birds, are preserved. In the visitors center, a film and exhibits show artifacts and explain what is known about the three cultures that built the mounds between 500 B.C. and 1300. From the center, a steep trail winds up the bluff. Small signs tell how the original inhabitants used all parts of the trees and shrubs that grow here.

Atop the bluff is the Little Bear Mounds, its rounded shape outlined in a band of gravel. Farther on is the Great Bear

Mound, 137 feet long and 3½ feet high. Once, mounds covered this area; because this blufftop site wasn't convenient for settlers, it was spared.

The river road then dips three miles to Marquette, an old rail junction in the shadow of the high bridge from Prairie du Chien. The most unusual sight in Marquette is the three-tier Port of Marquette Hotel, dramatically affixed to the vertical face of the bluff. Unfortunately, its view, which includes the *Miss Marquette* and the big restaurant linked to it by enclosed walkway, is reserved for guests.

The road to McGregor, occupying a sliver of flat land at the foot of the bluffs, is the most scenic of the stretch. And of the towns, McGregor is the most equipped for tourists, with its ornate Victorian houses, old brick storefronts and half-dozen antiques shops. An 1848 log cabin on Main Street, its small lawn filled with perennials, turns out to have a Jacuzzi and be part of the Little Switzerland Inn B&B next door, itself built in 1862 as home for the weekly *North Iowa Times*.

The true tourist attraction, however, has to be the River Junction Trade Co., an atmospheric general store that sells reproductions of clothing and goods from owner Jim Boeke's favorite era, 1870 to 1900—"the cowboy, the gunfighter and the riverboat gambler," Boeke says.

You think that gunpowder crate of rusty cattle brands is authentic? The crate is; the brands were painstakingly reproduced from originals, just like the spurs, felt Jesse James hats and piles of striped bibfront shirts. In the case of the silver badges for Pinkerton detectives, Apache Police and Mesilla, New Mexico marshals, they are made by the same company that made them 100 years ago.

If Boeke isn't at a trade show, where he outfits theme-park performers and frontier-era re-enactors across the nation, you'll see him at the shop dressed head to toe in his own wares.

Other oddities in McGregor include the Elf Cave, a little scene dug into the limestone bluff next to a gift shop, and the McGregor Historical Museum, which includes "paintings" made in bottles of colored sand by a local artist.

Just south of town is Pikes Peak State Park, 500 feet above where the Wisconsin River joins the Mississippi in a jumble of islands and sloughs. Those who stand at its overlooks become voyeurs of life on the vast river plain below, where trains inch across the water on bridges, barges and houseboats lie at anchor and fishing boats putter into marshy corners. Twelve miles of trails thread through ravines and forests in the park, chosen as a future fort by Zebulon Pike on the same 1805 trip that resulted in Fort Snelling. However, it was never settled.

A series of hills through bucolic farmland leads to Guttenberg, where frame houses alternate with thick, pre-Civil War limestone buildings that look as if they could hold off Sherman himself. From the gazebo or many benches and picnic tables on Guttenberg's riverfront park, or from the official observation platform, visitors can watch barges go through the locks.

On a hillside near the highway, a pair of painters have started a B&B and art gallery in a renovated 1858 brewery. Two guest rooms retain the 2-foot-thick stone walls, but the plumbing and decor is thoroughly modern. After she serves a big breakfast in a room that looks remarkably like a German *Weinkeller,* Pat Shahrivar gives tours of an underground limestone cave that has baby stalactities and stalagmites.

For a loop tour, cross to Wisconsin on the car ferry at Cassville, 11 miles south of Guttenberg, or continue on to Dubuque. The Wisconsin side of the river is scenic, too, though the road doesn't always hug the river as it does in Iowa.

Just don't try it on a bike.

❂ TRIP TIPS: Northeast Iowa

- **Accommodations:** FitzGerald's Inn B&B in Lansing, (319) 538-4872. From the 1863 house, a terraced lawn leads up to a screened gazebo that overlooks the river and bridge. Friendly proprietor and five rooms, $50–$75.

  Little Switzerland Inn B&B in McGregor, (319) 873-2057. Five rooms, $60–$80, and a log cabin, $100.

  McGregor Manor B&B in McGregor, (319) 873-2600. Four rooms in a restored 1897 home, $62–$72. Occasional mystery evenings.

  Old Brewery B&B in Guttenberg, (319) 252-2094. Two rooms, $55 and $60.

  Port of Marquette Hotel, (319) 873-3477. Twenty-four motel-style rooms, $74.

- **Dining:** Breitbach's, (319) 552-2220, in Balltown, 20 miles south of Guttenberg, is Iowa's oldest restaurant and is generally acknowledged to be the best in the area.

- **Boating:** The *Sand Cove Queen* in Lansing gives cruises of the wild-life-refuge backwaters at 7 P.M. Saturdays and 2 P.M. Sundays, May through October. (319) 538-4497.

    Boatels in McGregor, (800) 747-2628, rents houseboats, as does Lansing's C. Cruises, (319) 586-2287, and S&S Houseboat, (319) 538-4454.
- **Horseback tours:** SBJ Trail Rides in McGregor, (319) 873-2735.
- **Cave:** Seven miles west of McGregor is Spook Cave, which gives underground boat tours May through October. There's a campground, too, (319) 873-2144.
- **Car ferry:** The Cassville car ferry operates from 9 A.M. to 9 P.M. daily in summer, on weekends in May, September and October. Fare per car is $6 (608) 725-5180.
- **Events:** Lansing Fish Days, second weekend of August.

    Effigy Mounds moonlight tours, closest Saturday to full moon in June, July and August.

    McGregor holds a Spring Arts and Crafts Festival, Memorial Day weekend; Jesse James Trail Ride the fourth weekend in June and second weekend in September; Labor Day weekend parade and waterski show; Fall Arts and Crafts Festival, first full weekend in October; Leaf Lookers Arts and Crafts Festival and GRRRR walk and run, second weekend in October; and Feb Fab Fest, second full weekend in February.

    Guttenberg has its July Fest, weekend before the Fourth of July; and Germanfest, last weekend in September.
- **Information:** Lansing, (319) 538-4997; McGregor, (800) 896-0910; Guttenberg, (319) 252-2068 and (319) 252-2323; Pikes Peak State Park, (319) 873-2341; Effigy Mounds National Monument, (319) 873-3491.

Dubuque
Stone mansions and painted ladies

Walnut carpenter's lace. Fireplaces made of Italian mosaic tile. Yards of leaded glass and richly printed, century-old wallpaper.

Oooooohh.

That's what the two dozen people on a house tour and progressive dinner in Dubuque, Iowa, kept saying as the tour progressed from one Victorian mansion to another.

Despite its obvious appeal to the antiques crowd, the tour is more than a cavalcade of architecture and ostentation. Along the way emerges a social history of a frontier town in which an enterprising man could grab opportunity and turn it into enormous wealth.

Dubuque is the grittier cousin of Galena, 16 miles south in Illinois. Both sprang out of a lead-mining boom, but Galena, three miles distant from the Mississippi, started shrinking before the Civil War. Dubuque kept growing and producing—lumber, meat, wagons, boats—and prospering, which explains the abundance and variety of Victorian architecture.

French-Canadian fur trader Julien Dubuque was the first white man to settle in the area; he traded lead mined by local Mesquakies until his death in 1810. Missouri farmboy Mathias Ham set up shop after the ugly Blackhawk War of 1832 wrested control of the area from the Indians, and pulled millions of dollars in lead ore from the earth.

It is at Ham's 1856 blufftop house, now a museum, that the progressive dinner starts. My group settled around tables in the cellar for chicken salad in puff pastry and fruit. Then we joined interpreter Rachael Beasley, who started her commentary on upper-class social mores of the time by showing us a whalebone waist cincher—18 inches, about the circumference of a canteloupe—that girls were forced to wear starting from age 6 or 7.

The keeping of appearances turned out to be a recurring theme in the houses, which were built to impress business associates. Ham put a cupola and an eight-pillar entrance on his limestone-block house, but it didn't help his fortunes much—they soon changed, and he was forced to take in boarders.

Across town, at the Redstone Inn, we spooned up vegetable soup in the warm glow of walnut and redwood, under crystal-teardrop chandeliers. The man who built the 1894 mansion came to Dubuque in 1846 at age 17, and, from a job as a blacksmith's apprentice that paid $35 a year, built the Cooper Wagon and Buggy Co., supplier of the covered wagon known as Old Reliable, which took pioneers to Utah and along the Oregon Trail. A.A. Cooper built the Redstone as a wedding gift for his daughter; today, it's an inn.

The builder of the 1873 Ryan House, now a restaurant, earned his wealth the old-fashioned way—through connections. Meatpacker William Ryan had an influential friend from his Galena days, Gen. Ulysses S. Grant, and the result was contracts to supply the Union Army and frontier forts with pork.

We ate London broil and tarragon chicken as owner Janice Wagner regaled us with a history of the house and its strongwilled occupants over the years.

Then it was on to English trifle in the 1890 Stout House, a showcase of the kind of carpenter's artistry a lumber baron can command. Frank Stout made much of his fortune on Wisconsin's white pine, but chose Brazilian rosewood, sycamore, mahogany and blond oak from the Philippines for this house.

From the Stout House, it was only two blocks to my room at the 1908 Mandolin Inn, yet another fabulous old mansion that gets its name from a lovely leaded and painted-glass window portraying St. Cecilia, patron of musicians. A formal four-course breakfast was served the next morning with candlelight and soft concertos.

Then it was back to real life. The funny thing about Dubuque is, it doesn't feel much like real life—not modern days, anyway. In fact, it's often used as a movie setting, most recently filling in for Boston in *Field of Dreams*.

Economic stagnation after 1900, isolation from interstates and homogeneity of culture—Irish and German Catholics make up the bulk of the population—give the streets the feel of blue-collar Europe married to 1950s America. In some neighborhoods, nearly every corner has a bar; Dubuque has quite a reputation for beer consumption.

Like the houses, the most picturesque tourist attraction in town is rooted in the past. In 1882, a banker who lived atop the bluffs but worked below got fed up with the long buggy ride around the bluff, which ate into his noontime nap. So he built an incline railway, modeled after those in the Alps, and had his gardener haul him up in a cable car each noon. J.K. Graves' neighbors envied him and asked for rides; soon the railway was opened to the public.

Today, tourists love to creak up the 65 percent grade in the little green-and-white car. Locals use it, too, to get to the Saturday farmers market and the boutiques in Cable Car Square. The view of the river and steepled cityscape from above is magnificent.

On the bluffs sit many more Victorians, painted ladies rather than the red and brown stone mansions below. Banker Graves' frame house, with turret and curving porch, is among them on Fenelon Place.

Graves, Ham, Ryan, Cooper and Stout. They thought big and built big, and their landmarks ensure they're not forgotten.

❂ TRIP TIPS: Dubuque, Iowa

- **Victorian House Tour and Progressive Dinner:** June through December on Friday evenings, $36, with a Christmas edition that includes a reading from Dickens, $40. Call Dawn Wolf at (800) 226-3369. The Stout House now is a private home; the Mandolin Inn, a brick Queen Anne built by insurance and banking magnate Nicholas Schrup, has replaced it on the tour.
- **Events:** Dubuque Fest, third weekend in May.
  Catfish Festival, fourth weekend in June.
  Riverfest and Dragonboat Races, second weekend in September.
  Fall Festival, first full weekend in October.
  Candlelight Christmas House Tour, early December.
- **Downhill skiing:** Sundown Ski Area just outside town, (319) 556-6676.
- **Other attractions:** Diamond Jo Casino, Grand Opera House, River Museum complex. The Fenelon Place Elevator is open April through November.
- **Accommodations:** Victorian inns include the Mandolin Inn, $55–$125, (800) 524-7996; Hancock House, $75–$150, (319) 557-8989; Redstone Inn, $60–$175; (319) 582-1894; and Richards House, $40–$95, (319) 557-1492.
- **Information:** (800) 798-8844.

Galena

Booming again after a long sleep

In the grand scheme of things, Galena, Illinois, was destined to be a flash in the pan.

The flash came from the shiny lead sulfide upon which the

town's fortunes were built in the 1830s, '40s and '50s; *galena* is the Latin word for the ore. It made many people rich, and in the 1850s, Galena, three miles from the Mississippi, was the busiest port between St. Paul and St. Louis.

The new railroad approached, but the steamboat lines made sure it stayed away from Galena. Then the lead market weakened, trade routes shifted and the town's steep hillsides, which had given up their trees for the smelting furnaces and their limestone for houses, began to erode into the Galena River. By 1910, the river had shrunk so much the steamboats couldn't get through.

Galena settled into obscurity. But its luster began to return in the 1960s, when people looked around and saw a town that wasn't just old, but antique. On Main Street were rows and rows of brick storefronts. High above on "Quality Hill," and across the now-puny river, were rows of Italianate mansions and Queen Annes and Greek Revivals.

Well, everyone's seen nice houses. But what sets Galena's architecture apart is what's not there: no concrete boxes, no plywood facades, barely anything built in the 20th century, except a Carnegie library and the old hilltop high school, now condos. Galena's residents simply couldn't afford to replace anything.

Today, a walk through this town is a joy. Houses and storefronts have been restored, though not to an unholy perfection. Spring bulbs bloom willy-nilly in hillside crevices; children careen through town on skates.

Along Main Street, fancy shops sell cappuccino, pottery, lacy baby dresses, hand-painted toy soldiers and all kinds of antiques.

Four inns occupy historic buildings, including the DeSoto House, whose wrought-iron balcony is hung with red, white and blue bunting in memory of 1856, when Abraham Lincoln spoke from it, and 1868, when Gen. Ulysses Grant ran his successful presidential campaign out of the hotel.

Hugging the hillside above downtown is Bench Street, home to B&Bs, the Galena/Jo Daviess County History Museum and four of the churches whose white steeples contribute so much to the town's skyline. The really fine mansions, three of them guest houses, are a huff and a puff higher, on Prospect Street.

This historic district is best seen from across the river in pleasant Grant Park, reached by footbridge. Here is a statue of the great man, who was not so great in 1860, when, having resigned from the Army, he came to Galena to work as a clerk in his father's leather shop. When war broke out, Grant formed a volunteer company of locals and began drilling them.

Two years later, he was commander-in-chief of the Union Army. In another two years, he returned to Galena's huzzahs and a house bought for him by local businessmen. Today, the Grant Home is open for tours, with almost all of its original furnishings.

This peaceful part of Galena also contains houses that have a variety of histories and architectural styles, explained on one-hour Galena Trolley Tours. Guides toss out interesting historical tidbits, of which Galena seems to have a limitless supply: For example, Gen. Grant, who died of throat cancer, smoked more than 20 footlong cigars a day and was given 10,000 boxes of cigars by a tobacco company after the war.

Galena had a short heyday, but the town packed a lot into it. The characters it produced, including nine Civil War generals and one accused traitor, provide plenty of grist for Galenians. Paul LeGreco, who sells pewter soldiers at his Toy Shops of Galena, impersonates Grant at his shop. Folk singer Jim Post portrays Mark Twain and other figures at the Trolley Depot Theatre. Lucy Miele plays Southern belle Julia Dent Grant in "Tea and Tarts With the General's Lady," at the DeSoto House and around town.

Not surprisingly, all this history and charm attracts tourists. Galena's current population is 3,500, but weekend visitors push it back toward and sometimes past its 1858 peak of 14,000.

May and the first half of June is the best time to visit; in summer and fall, the streets can be uncomfortably crowded.

Apparently, this old flash in the pan has plenty of flash left.

❂ TRIP TIPS: Galena, Ill.

- **Events:** Farmers' market, Saturday mornings at the Old Market House, mid-May through October.
  Spring Tour of Homes, second weekend in June.
  Galena Arts Festival, third weekend in July.
  Fall Tour of Homes, fourth weekend in September.

Galena Country Fair and Civil War Living History Encampment, first full weekend in October.

Historic Cemetery Walk, second weekend in October.

- **Tours:** Galena Trolley Tours, 314 S. Main St., cost $8, $10 and $15, depending on stops, and run all year. (815) 777-1248.
- **Nightlife:** Jim Post performs one-man shows at the Trolley Depot Theatre, (815) 777-1248, all year. And there's usually music being performed in the bistros along Main Street.
- **Accommodations:** For weekends, book far in advance. There are many nice inns, B&Bs and cottages; call for a Visitor's Guide. The ideal thing to do is arrive midweek at the visitors center, just across the river in the old railroad depot, and leaf through its photo album of inns; $75–$95 is average. Midweek is cheapest. Many smaller establishments have a two-night minimum on peak weekends. The DeSoto House, while convenient, is overpriced at $95–$175.
- **Dining:** Vinny Vanucchi's, 201 S. Main St., has a pleasant outdoor patio, friendly service and inexpensive food. Jackels' Backerei & Cafe, 200 S. Main St., is a good place to have coffee and pastries.
- **Information:** Galena/Jo Daviess County Convention and Visitors Bureau, (800) 747-9377.

Cave Country
Exploring two limestone labyrinths

The gravel road winds sedately through the farmland of southeastern Minnesota, past barns and fields. Iowa is a mile away, with more barns, more fields.

You'd never guess that Paul Bunyan's Bed is 200 feet below the surface.

This is Minnesota's cave country—geologically speaking, karst country, an area of porous limestone cut through by underground streams and linked to the surface by sinkholes. Local farmers simply plowed around them until, one day in 1924, three pigs disappeared from a farm near Harmony. The farmer, looking for his missing pigs, found a sinkhole and sent some neighbor boys down by rope. Seventy-five feet later, they found the pigs—still alive—and a huge labyrinth of underground canyons, formed by eons of water zigzagging through the rock that lies under the cornstalks.

Tours began at Niagara Cave in 1934; the pigs' landing spot is called the Reception Room. Tours today probably haven't changed much; they're richly kitschy, with goofy metal signs marking each new thrill.

While privately owned Niagara honors the golly-gee awe that must have been felt by its young discoverers, nearby Mystery Cave is the cave those neighbor boys would have found had they gone off to MIT and come back with degrees in mineralogy.

Mystery Cave was discovered on a frigid day in 1937 by a man walking along the south branch of the Root River. Because the air inside the cave is 48 degrees year-round, it had melted the snow on the ground around a sinkhole, and steam was rising from it. The man got a ladder, a rope and a light, and voila! Tours started 10 years later, and the Minnesota Department of Natural Resources bought the cave in 1988. Today, naturalists lead tours of parts of the 12 miles of passages, flicking electronic switches as they go and pointing out formations with the red pinpoint of a laser.

The terrain above the two caves includes the picturesque valleys and ridges of bluff country. Lanesboro is the tourist hub, with new restaurants and B&Bs opening on the strength of the town's spot on the popular Root River State Trail. Preston also is connected to the trail and is closest to Forestville State Park, which includes miles of horse trails and Historic Forestville, where costumed interpreters re-enact the summer of 1899. Harmony has capitalized on its Amish neighbors; two tour companies take the curious to Amish farms, and country-crafts shops sell Amish wares.

Echoing the limestone labyrinths underneath, a maze of pretty county roads connects the towns.

People from all over the world bump along County Road 30 south of Harmony to see Niagara Cave; on the late-June day we visit, the guest book holds entries from Mexico, Thailand and Japan. From the road, only a white-frame house can be seen; inside is a half-hearted souvenir shop, a few plastic snack tables and a white metal door.

Holly Koliha, a local high-school student, gathers her group, opens the door and leads us down a steep flight of stairs. "Aw, cool!" exclaims a boy as water drips on our heads and we enter the Reception Room, once the juncture of two glacial streams. From there, Koliha leads us to a domed room with a 60-foot waterfall, which we view looking down from a small platform with thin rails.

"My niece says it looks like Disney made it," an Iowa woman tells me. My young daughter, shrinking away, thinks the deep pit looks all too authentic.

Niagara Cave's natural formations beg to be presented with a sense of whimsy, and its owners have happily complied. Koliha leads us next to the "alligator's back," a long mound of deeply pocked rock that she says covered the cave floor before developers leveled it. Next is the wedding chapel, where we all sit on white plastic benches, used as pews, while Holly points out the "steeple" behind us and the "fireplace" to the right.

The chapel, predictably, is dank and depressing, but it's been used for more than 300 weddings. "You'd certainly limit the guests that way," chimes the Iowa woman.

Not far away is the ledge where Paul Bunyan took a nap—apparently, he was 15 feet tall with the waist and hip measurements of Miss America—and his saddle, which does look exactly like a saddle. Then we see the Elephant Head, with a draped gray ear and wrinkled trunk. The three-layer Wedding Cake, with icing dripping over its top. The Mighty Mo, with the jutting prow of the battleship *Missouri,* and the Liberty Bell, complete with crack.

Along with the fun, Koliha sneaks in quite a bit of geology. She points out the fossil of a 450-million-year-old sponge embedded in the wall. She explains the different types of stalactites, and the rate at which they're formed: 1 cubic inch per 100 years. She points out chert, a rock that juts out of the wall like bone joints, used by Indians to make cutting utensils.

The Iowa woman, though, has Hollywood on the brain. "It's just like *Journey to the Center of the Earth,*" she remarks. "Like *Indiana Jones and the Temple of Doom.*"

It's not a stretch to think so. Ribbon stalactites, formed by ancient rivulets of water, look just like skeletal fingers; pebbles bouncing in long-ago streams have bored holes into the rock that often resemble the sunken eye sockets of a skull.

By the time we get to Mystery Cave, 20 miles away, our imaginations are stoked to a high blast. As naturalist Maryanne Ewalt leads our group along, talking about organic acids and chemical reactions, I suddenly see the outline of Zeus in the rock, his cheeks filled with wind. Then a rainbow trout. A conch shell. The pipes of an organ.

Formations get short shrift here, but Ewalt has other interesting things to impart. We are walking on an ancient sea floor, she says, once silty muck, now rock. She points out fossils of cephalopods, 15- to 20-foot-long mollusks that were the forerunners of today's octopus and squid.

Today, four species of bats live in the cave, coming and going through a window cut above its vaultlike door. Ewalt explains how female bats catch their newborns in a pouch; how sleeping bats, if disturbed, need half an hour to raise their metabolism enough to fly; how bats can eat a third of their body weight in mosquitoes every night.

After Niagara, the cave seems almost obsessively polished. Its concrete walkways are dry and smooth, with a little rolled rim. Lights along the passages flick off after a few minutes, like those in cheap European hotels, because the DNR wants to limit the growth of moss from outside spores. Twice, stragglers are dunked in darkness; luckily, it's a mellow group, and nobody panics.

Despite its preservation efforts, I wonder if the DNR leveled the ceiling, which seems suspiciously flat. But Ewalt explains that it is natural, formed by the settling of sheets of limestone between layers of shale.

Without fanfare, we next come upon Turquoise Lake, shimmering blue and serene 130 feet below the surface. It's so perfect I almost feel I've seen it before, perhaps in my imagination.

As it turns out, the show isn't over for me and my daughter. As we drive away from Mystery Cave, I see a doe start across the gravel road, and I stop. With a doubtful look at us, she continues, fetches a fawn from the tall grass and heads back. But before returning to the woods, she stops and nurses the fawn.

We watch, enthralled. In cave country, there's something interesting around every corner.

☻ TRIP TIPS: Cave country

- **Tours:** At Niagara Cave, hourlong tours are given weekends in May, September and October and daily from Memorial Day to Labor Day. Cost is $6 for adults, $3.75 for children 5–12. Call (507) 886-6606.

  Hourlong tours of Mystery Cave are given weekends from mid-April to Memorial Day, daily until Labor Day, then weekends through October. On summer holidays and weekends, tours are given of another section of the caves, known as Minnesota Caverns, where visitors carry hand-held lanterns. Visitors caravan from Mystery Cave to the entrance; allow 1 1/2 to two hours.

  Mystery Cave is handicapped-accessible. It is five miles west of Forestville State Park. Cost for each tour is $5 for adults, $3 children 5–12. A $4 state-park sticker also is required. Call (507) 937-3251.

  Bring a jacket and wear comfortable, water-resistant walking shoes.

- **Accommodations:** Midpoint between the two caves is Preston, where the 1869 JailHouse Inn B&B, (507) 765-2181, offers 12 attractive rooms, including a cellblock with bars, that rent for $40–$140.

Old Barn Resort, (507) 467-2512, is just off the Root River Trail between Lanesboro and Fountain. It has a restaurant, hostel ($10–$14 per person), campground and heated pool and rents bikes, in-line skates and canoes.

To reserve campsites in Forestville State Park, call the Connection at (612) 922-9000, (800) 246-2267. The park is at (507) 352-5111.

• **Amish farm tours:** Michels Amish Tours, (800) 752-6474, and Amish Country Tours, (507) 886-2303.

• **Information:** Historic Bluff Country, (800) 792-5833; Lanesboro, (800) 944-2670.

Lanesboro
A picturesque hamlet with a past

A farm where tools are mysteriously spirited to new locations. A blufftop wracked by the disembodied scream of a child. A young Indian woman who glides down the Root River in a birchbark canoe, singing a haunting song—as she has for centuries.

Isolated Lanesboro is a wholesome little hamlet, but it's got a colorful past that hasn't quite passed away. See that bicycle trail slicing through downtown, the one crowded with tourists in bright Spandex? In 1870, it was a brand-new railroad line. One night that October, the crew of a train approaching Lanesboro suddenly saw an Indian man in its headlights, standing on the tracks and holding up his hand. They couldn't help running over the man but, when they backed up, could find no traces of the body.

This happened again and again, until a local Winnebago chief explained it was a father, seeking help for a boy who had drowned in the river long ago. And until the last train went through in 1973, engineers tooted the horn at that spot, whether they saw the man or not.

Every Saturday in the fall, innkeeper Duke Addicks tells these stories and others by candlelight in Lanesboro's old Sons of Norway lodge. Over the years, Addicks has become a magnet for strange stories.

"People come up to me and say, 'We've never told anybody about this, but . . .'" Addicks told his rapt audience. "There's probably ghosts around you. You just have to be kind of attuned to them."

Actually, Lanesboro is one of the liveliest, least sepulchral towns in the Midwest on summer and fall weekends, when it's filled to the gills with tourists. It's come full circle: The four-story Phoenix Hotel was the largest hotel west of the Mississippi in the late 1860s, thanks to land speculators who envisioned a spa town on the site, hemmed in on three sides by tall limestone bluffs. Instead, Lanesboro, population 850, slowly declined until the gorgeous Root River State Trail finally brought mobs to its century-old storefronts.

One October, I joined the influx of tourists. It was Octoberfest, and there was a happy hubbub at Das Wurst Haus, where owner Arv Fabian was working up a sweat on the concertina behind the sausage case, with his wife, Jan, on piano, and son, John, on tuba. Customers hooted and clapped as waitresses carried bratwurst and Schell's beer to Formica tables under acoustical tile: the look of the Midwest, but the spirit of Munich.

At the Lanesboro History Museum, Doris Peterson was presiding over a parade of people who came to look at town memorabilia, such as the 1911 megaphone used to announce local ski tournaments and the totem-like walking stick of Johnnie Rank, the town rattlesnake-catcher.

In Sylvan Park, an Amish woman was snapping up the sides of her buggy after selling her baked goods at the weekly farmers market. "Seems I never leave here with anything but jams and jellies," she commented, flashing a deep dimple.

A customer had fallen in love with a wood collage at Cornucopia Art Center, an artists' cooperative that also gives workshops. The Scenic Valley Winery was full of people sampling fruit wines: a cherry, sweet as Kool-Aid, and a more robust wild plum and raspberry.

By 7:30 P.M., the lobby of the Commonweal Theater was full of people awaiting a performance of Euripides' *Medea*. Giggling young girls were walking arm-in-arm up Parkway Avenue from the Community Center, where polka bands had been playing all day. I went there after the ghost stories and danced a few waltzes with gregarious dairy farmer Elton Redalen, who knew everything about the area. He told me where to see crowds of wild turkeys—"Go to Inspiration Peak off Highway 16 in early morning or at dusk; it's unbelievable, all the wildlife"—and suggested I have Sunday brunch at the nearby Forest Resource Center.

At the environmental learning center, deep in the hills northwest of town, cooks dished up biscuits with sausage gravy, French toast, bacon, hashbrowns and scrambled eggs with shiitake mushrooms. After brunch, naturalist Karla Kinstler led the group down a wooded hill to the shiitake operation, showing us where ironwood logs are inoculated with mushroom "spawn," watered, rested, soaked and left to fruit. It takes more than a year, but the center gets $8.50 a pound for the intensely flavored mushrooms.

Then it was on to the Treetops High Ropes Course, a series of 30-feet-high cables strung between towers on the bluff above the North Arm of the Root. "It does get your adrenaline going," Kinstler acknowledged.

The view was stupendous—and so was the terror inspired by the Apple Picker, which forced us to walk sideways on a cable, pulling ourselves from one short knotted rope to another. "I would never have guessed I'd be doing something like this," my ropes buddy, Larry, said grimly as he finished it.

Haunted houses, hoedowns and high-wire acts—it's just another fall weekend in Lanesboro.

⚙ TRIP TIPS: Lanesboro and trail towns

- **Events:** Sykkle Tur, festivities in all trail towns, third weekend in May.
  Trail Days in Fountain, first weekend in June.
  Art in the Park in Lanesboro, Father's Day.
  Buffalo Bill Days in Lanesboro, first weekend in August.
  Oktoberfest in Lanesboro, first Saturday in October.
  "Who Haunts Here?" Saturdays, August through October.
  Christmas Along the Trail tour of inns, first weekend in December.
  Candlelight skiing on the Root River Trail out of Whalan, January and February.
- **Nightlife:** The Commonweal Theater puts on professional productions Memorial Day through Christmas, (800) 657-7025.
- **Forest Resource Center:** The ropes course, open all year, is $5. Call (507) 467-2437 for a schedule of events.

•**Accommodations:** From May through October, rooms are scarce on weekends; the tourism office can help locate vacancies. Among the inns are:

Cottage House Inn, (800) 944-0099, across from the theater, offers classic hospitality and simple but fine rooms, $45–$60. It also rents the Riverside Homestead, a nearby house, $100 for two adults, children under 12 free.

Green Gables Inn, (507) 467-2936, is a newly built motel on Highway 16, 13 rooms, $45–$75. Good for families with kids.

Mrs. B's is a well-run B&B in an 1872 building downtown. Ten rooms, $50–$95, (800) 657-4710.

The 1890 Cady Hayes House is a lovely Queen Anne in a Lanesboro neighborhood. Three rooms, $60–$105, (507) 467-2621.

Brewster's Red Hotel, is in an 1870s building downtown, right next to the trail, and has pleasant rooms, $45–$65, but no common areas. (507) 467-2998 or (507) 467-2999.

The Wenneson Hotel in Peterson is a beautifully restored 1904 railroad hotel, four rooms and suite, $50–$90. (507) 875-2587.

The Meadows Inn, on a hillside overlooking Rushford, was built in 1993 but resembles a European country chateau. Five rooms, $75–$125. (507) 864-2378.

• **Dining:** The Old Village Hall in downtown Lanesboro has a pleasant deck and serves very good grilled meats, pastas and salads; Mrs. B's offers multicourse dinners by reservation only. The Victorian House serves food from the Alsace-Lorraine region of France. For a picnic with a view, pick up lunch at the Picnic Basket in Lanesboro and take it to Inspiration Peak, off Highway 16 between Lanesboro and Preston.

• **Information:** Lanesboro Tourism, (800) 944-2670.

Decorah
Still Norwegian after all these years

In northeast Iowa, in a natural bowl surrounded by wooded ridges and limestone-pocked bluffs, immigrants from Norway in the 1850s and '60s found their vesterheim—their home in the west.

They settled into Decorah with a vengeance, starting a Norwegian-language newspaper in 1874 and then, in 1877, a museum to preserve the heritage of the old country. There weren't that many of them—Decorah has just 8,700 residents today—but they were proud, and they were determined to hang onto their heritage.

Today, not much has changed, except, every year at the end of July, their descendants and everyone else who lives in Decorah spend three hectic days manning lefse and lutefisk booths. That's because a mob of 40,000 to 60,000 descends on the town for Nordic Fest, a cultural lovefest of rosemaling, wood-carving, old-time dancing and krumkake-munching and a kind of homecoming for Norwegians from many states.

Decorah claims top billing as the center of Norwegian-American culture through a triple whammy: Luther College, established by Norwegians in 1861; the *Decorah Posten,* published in Norwegian for nearly a century, until 1972; and Vesterheim, a 14-building complex that claims to be the nation's most comprehensive museum dedicated to a single immigrant group.

As a member of a household in which there usually is a cube of gjetost cheese getting old in the fridge, I thought it would be fun to pay homage. We started at Vesterheim, where exhibits follow the progress of the immigrants: from the dark, rough old-country homes to ship models, the contents of a typical immigrant's trunk—iron, cloth, candlestick, spindle, china cup, kettle—and the new homes in America.

One such cabin, built in 1852–53 from a single pine tree in Big Canoe, Iowa, now rests on the museum's second floor. The homesickness of the immigrants can be felt in the basement, which holds intricate wooden models carved on long winter nights: a 12th-century stave church, and a stunning altar inspired by baroque ones in Norway. In warm months, tours are given of outside buildings, which include an 1851 stone mill, a blacksmith shop and a limestone church.

Next door is the Dayton House, which specializes in Norwegian dishes. We had its Sunday-morning smorgasbord, ignoring the hard bread, herring and Havarti in favor of waffles with fresh strawberries and blueberries. I did have cup after cup of one authentic Scandinavian item, the superb coffee.

Decorah's main thoroughfare, Water Street, is lined with benches decorated with rosemaling; other than that, it could be any prosperous lineup of century-old brick and frame commercial buildings. We stopped and spent an hour at Vanberia, a very fine Scandinavian-imports shop.

We strayed from the heritage tour to see the waterfall in Dunning's Spring Park, a shady, secluded pocket of greenery where a troll walk is held during Nordic Fest. Then we drove up from downtown to a national historic district of houses and, at its edge, Phelps Park, with more trails. Along the bluff, we walked along a stone pathway covered with vine-entwined arbors to a romantic stone gazebo, overlooking the winding path of the Upper Iowa River.

We drove home savoring the distinctive geography of bluff country, swooping down long stretches of road and up again, through rolling pastures broken by woods and limestone outcroppings. Twelve miles north of Decorah, we turned off into tiny Burr Oak, where a 9-year-old Laura Ingalls Wilder and her family spent a year in 1876–77 managing a hotel. Wilder never wrote about that year in Burr Oak, where her sister Grace was born, and in her famous "Little House" books, she never mentioned the infant brother who died on the trip there.

Pa Ingalls' hotel has been renovated into the Laura Ingalls Wilder Museum, which has become a stop on the tourist route that follows the family's travels from Pepin, Wisconsin, to De Smet, South Dakota. Now, Burr Oak—until recently a mere blip in the road—also is the home of Burr Oak Mercantile and Country Cafe, next door, plus an art gallery and a potter's studio and shop.

As in Decorah, the settlers of long ago have left an indelible mark on the landscape.

✪ TRIP TIPS: Decorah

- **Events:** Nordic Fest, the last full weekend in July. Reservations at inns and motels in Decorah are practically a family heirloom, but there are rooms in nearby motels, private homes in Decorah and at Luther College; call (800) 382-3378 as soon as possible.

  At Vesterheim, Velkommen is the first Saturday in May; Norwegian Food Fest, first weekend in October; Norwegian Christmas, first weekend in December. Call (319) 382-9681.

  Luther College's Nordic Choir is one of the nation's top a cappella college choruses; the orchestra and concert band also are top-notch. For a monthly list of concerts, theater performances, lectures and faculty recitals, call (319) 387-1865. For the yearly Calendar of Events, call (319) 387-1291.

- **Laura Ingalls Wilder Museum in Burr Oak:** Open May 1 through mid-October.
- **Accommodations:** Reserve in advance, because festivals and special events at Luther College can fill the town.

  Motels include the Heartland Inn, (319) 382-2269, and Cliff House, (800) 632-5980; the B&Bs are Montgomery Mansion, (800) 892-4955; Victoria Cottage, (319) 382-4897; Broadway B&B, (319) 382-2329.
- **Information:** Decorah Area Chamber of Commerce, (800) 463-4692.

☢ TRIP TIPS: Visiting Spillville

Spillville, 12 miles southwest, is famous for hosting Czech composer Antonin Dvorak during the summer of 1893 and for the fabulous carved clocks at the Bily Clock Exhibit, which also houses a Dvorak museum.

- **Accommodations:** Old World Inn, (319) 562-3739, has four pleasant rooms, $55–$75. Its restaurant is open daily April–October, Thursday–Sunday in the winter.

  Taylor-Made B&B, (319) 562-3958, has four bedrooms, $69.
- **Events:** Dvorak's Birthday Celebration and Concert, early September.
- **Bily exhibit:** The museum is open daily from April through October, winter weekends and by appointment, (319) 562-3569. Admission is $3 for adults, $1.25 for children 7 to 12.

5 MINNESOTA'S PIONEER PRAIRIE

New Ulm
Forest gnomes and Teutonic warriors

In city and village squares across Germany at the start of Advent, the curtain goes up on thousands of brightly lit, pine-trimmed stalls selling ornaments, toys, sweets and other goods—the open-air Christ-child markets, a holiday tradition for centuries. As a collector of blown-glass Central European ornaments, I'd love to see them.

But Munich is 5,000 miles away; New Ulm, whose slogan is "Discover Germany in Minnesota," is a short drive. So my family and I drove down one winter evening. The season's first flakes of snow skittered out of the darkness and across our windshield, putting us in the mood for an excursion to, as a billboard announced, "The Christmas City."

We settled into the Holiday Inn, a sprawling complex with a half-timbered look, and soon were eating sauerbraten and spaetzle with gravy in its Heidelberg restaurant.

In the morning, I knew just where to go: Domeiers German store, a tiny shop in a residential neighborhood. I stepped from the quiet street into a gentle cacophony of accordion music and cuckoo clocks, clicking and twittering from their perches all over the store, cheek by jowl with nutcrackers, Nativity figures, nesting dolls, gnomes and rows and rows of gleaming glass ornaments.

I saw some old favorites and some new prizes, and soon I had an assistant running to and fro to fetch them: a rosy-cheeked forest elf playing an accordion; a grinning black cat; a pot-bellied gnome; a green-and-red village chapel with a gold onion dome, its roof crusted with glitter snow.

After making my picks, I stocked up on Advent calendars, brandy-filled chocolates and gaily decorated candies for my daughter's Christmas stocking. As Marlene Domeier was totting up my purchases, throwing in a red blown-glass mushroom for good measure, the door swung open and a woman shouted, "I've got 30 aboard!" Domeier shot back, "We can take 20." A tour bus stood outside, and in an instant, the little store was filled. Tip: Don't bring small children.

Then it was time for sightseeing, and the whole family headed up a narrow, winding road through the woods above town to Schell's. A working brewery, its picturesque grounds include August Schell's 1885 brick mansion with gingerbread trim, a vine-covered brick gift shop and a small museum, set on grounds that include statuary, pergolas and a gazebo under which painted gnomes play cards.

The 1860 brewery adjoins Flandrau State Park, where it holds a hunt for carved goat heads during Bockfest late every winter. The park has hilltop trails and a swimming area, and during World War II was the site of a German prisoner of war camp.

From Schell's, we drove along Summit Avenue, admiring the view of the town below, to the 1897 Hermann monument, an enormous statue of the tribal warrior who routed the Romans from the Teutoberg Forest in A.D. 9—though probably not with the help of the winged helmet he wears in New Ulm. In the summer, visitors can climb the pedestal for 50 cents and picnic in the pavilions at Hermann's feet.

In the downtown below, we went prowling for more jewels from Bavarian glass workshops. The Christmas Haus on Minnesota Street has a maze of 11 rooms with themes—Italian creches, Victorian dolls, Scandinavian items, country crafts, excruciatingly ugly Taiwanese ornaments—and I was about to turn heel when I glimpsed one more room. It turned out to be the German room, with steins and kitschy refrigerator magnets ("You can always tell a German, but you can't tell him much"), but also a tree loaded with hand-painted glass ornaments and a very good collection of nutcrackers. On the wall was a display that shows how ornaments are made.

We could have kept going, but our budget had limits. On the way home, we stopped by the Sausage Shop and the Backerei, where we picked up some sauerkraut rye bread and hard rolls.

We had the rolls for breakfast the next day, European-style with butter and jam. While they didn't really measure up to brotchen, the crusty rolls we love so much in Germany, they were, like New Ulm itself, the next best thing.

☻ TRIP TIPS: New Ulm

- **Events:** Fasching at Turner Hall and Bockfest at Schell's Brewery, the Saturday before Ash Wednesday.
  Heritagefest, second and third weekends in July.
  Oktoberfest, first and second weekends in October.
  Parade of Lights, the Friday after Thanksgiving, and Christmas festivities at the Brown County Museum, downtown shops and Schell's Brewery; call for a schedule.
- **Schell's brewery tours:** Daily from Memorial Day to Labor Day. (507) 354-5528.
- **Museums:** The Brown County Historical Museum, (507) 354-2016, is a striking brick Renaissance building. The 1887 Lind House was the home of Minnesota's 14th governor; the 1894 Wanda Gag house was the childhood home of the children's-book author and illustrator.
- **Shopping:** Domeiers, 1020 S. Minnesota St., is open daily except Wednesday. (507) 354-4231.
- **Accommodations:** For Heritagefest and Oktoberfest, reserve far in advance. The Holiday Inn at the edge of town, (507) 359-2941, has a pool and a German restaurant, $69–$122.
- **Information:** New Ulm chamber, (507) 354-4217.

Minnesota River Valley

In 1862, a collision of cultures

Mrs. Jane Duerr sat in the shade of a tree beside a twig basket of eggs and dried apples, waiting for the agency physician to return.

She had come to the Lower Sioux Agency on the ferry that day in hopes of trading eggs for camphor, to give her young son relief for a "full head." As we sat beside her on the grass, Mrs. Duerr told us how she and her family had journeyed from Indiana, lured by newspaper accounts of opportunity in the area. They were making do with a garden and a field of corn, she said, and things were looking up: Her carpenter husband hoped to find work for the government, building 15 houses for Indians who had agreed to farm.

"The Indians are gathering now," she noted. "They expect an annuity any day now."

The year was 1861, and the Indians' annuity payment was made on time a week later, an event observed by Henry Thoreau and other tourists who took an excursion steamer from St. Paul to see the scenery and the colorful gathering of 5,000 Indians. Crops were growing well, and there had been a surplus the year before.

The doctor presumably came that day in mid-June; we'll never know, because we re-entered 1995 after we left Mrs. Duerr, a composite settler who, at the end of the day, became Jill McNutt, assistant site manager of the Lower Sioux Agency Historic Site.

We do know that, little more than a year later, Dr. Philander P. Humphrey was dead, along with his wife and two children—killed across the river from the agency as they fled a party of Dakota braves on Aug. 18, 1862, the first day of what today is called the U.S.-Dakota Conflict.

"For the people who settled north of the river, it was like a thunderbolt out of clear skies," says McNutt. "It was not expected at all."

In the next six weeks, at least 360 settlers were killed. No one knows how many Dakota were killed fighting U.S. soldiers, about 90 of whom died, but it ended that December with the hanging of 38 warriors at Mankato, the cancellation of all treaties and debts and the banishment of all Dakota from Minnesota.

Today, the beautiful stretch of the Minnesota River between Mankato and Granite Falls holds many reminders of the conflict, which sent shock waves through white settlements hundreds of miles away but now is

DAVE HARDMAN/PIONEER PRESS

largely forgotten outside communities of Dakota, who lost everything and remember it very well.

By rights, the trail starts in St. Peter, home of the Traverse des Sioux Treaty Site History Center. The museum was built on the site where bands of the Upper Sioux accepted a 20-mile-wide reservation along the river in return for their lands, signing a document that promised yearly payments but also allowed traders to siphon off large portions.

Instead, my family and I set out for Thoreau's destination, the Lower Sioux Agency near Redwood Falls. There, an interpretive center tells the history of the Dakotas' struggle to co-exist with whites and the events that led to the 1862 war. By then, the reservation had been reduced to a 10-mile-wide stretch south of the river in an 1858 treaty, which had provisions as unfavorable as those in the first treaties.

It is Children's Day at the site; volunteers are playing pow-wow music and telling stories, teaching kids how to count to 10 in Lakota and showing them how to make sponge prints and paint Dakota symbols. There is wild rice and pemmican, a pungent mixture of dried meat, fat and dried fruit, and wonderful fry bread and wojapi, a berry spread.

We walk down a path and meet Mrs. Duerr, who is sitting next to a stone warehouse that was to be the only building at either Upper or Lower agencies to survive the war.

The summer of 1861 was not a good one after all. Crops failed, and the winter was harsh. By June 1862, the Dakota were starving, but they put off their annual buffalo hunt in the West to wait for the annuity payment. But it was late, held up in a Washington drained by the Civil War. At the Lower Sioux Agency, an arrogant new agent refused to release all of the food and other provisions due until the gold also arrived.

In one of the tragic ironies that run throughout the conflict, the gold had nearly reached Fort Ridgely, two months late, when four young braves, on a dare over the theft of eggs, shot and killed five settlers 40 miles north of the river, in Acton.

Despite the prophecies of their eloquent leader, Little Crow—"The white men are like the locusts when they fly so thick that the whole sky is a snowstorm . . . kill one, two, 10, and 10 times 10 will come to kill you"—the Dakota, already in trouble, decided to try to drive out the settlers. They attacked the Lower Sioux Agency the next day, killing 20 and plundering and burning buildings.

As we leave the site, we pass a grassy meadow studded with signs marking the locations of the trading posts, including that of Andrew Myrick, the trader who said, "Let them eat grass," and whose body was found with its mouth stuffed with grass. There is only one trading post operating now: the Lower Sioux Trading Post down the road, and next to it Jackpot Junction, both owned by the Mdewakanton band of Dakota, who eventually trickled back to Minnesota.

We check into the Dakota Inn, also run by the band, and briefly switch on the TV; it's a Bugs Bunny cartoon featuring an Indian with a target painted on his bare stomach. "Sh-You-Be-Um-Quiet," he says. "I-Hunt-Um-Rabbit." We switch it off and go to the pool, which has the band's symbol painted on its bottom—a butterfly, which we have learned at the agency means everlasting life.

In the cool of late afternoon, we drive north across the river to Birch Coulee. A solitary stone in a sea of tall grass marks where Dakota warriors surprised a burial party sent from Fort Ridgely, besieging it in a battle that became the biggest setback for U.S. troops.

At Jackpot Junction that evening, we eat in the restaurant and then use a hotel coupon to get a free $10 in quarters. I try my hardest to lose it at video poker, but everything comes up flushes. The man next to me is losing, but he's philosophical. "Might as well give some back to the Indians," he says.

The next day, we visit Alexander Ramsey Park, a former state park, in Redwood Falls. A plaque at its picturesque waterfall explains that city founder Col. Samuel McPhail first saw the area during a scouting expedition in 1862, and that it's named "redwood" because the Dakota daubed red paint on the trees to show that blood would flow if the Chippewa, who in the previous century had run the Dakota off their homeland in northern Minnesota, hunted there.

We pick up the trail again north of the river, and along County Road 15 find the most evocative part of the route. As we drive, we read to each other from history books and listen to the haunting mandolin and guitar music of Peter Ostroushko's "Heart of the Heartland," parts of which were written for public television's "The Dakota Conflict."

Here, on this isolated gravel road that hugs the lush river plain, we see how beautiful the valley is, and understand how the Dakota must have ached at losing it. We pass the Schwandt Memorial, at the end of a driveway that leads to a tidy white farmhouse, commemorating the deaths of six German settlers and their children on the first day of the war.

We pass a wood sculpture "dedicated to the pioneers who settled this valley," and after County Road 15 turns into 81, come to the Joseph R. Brown site. Brown, a capable former Indian agent who spoke fluent Dakota, had just built a three-story stone house on a hill overlooking the valley when, on the second day of the war, his Dakota wife and 12 children were captured and his house destroyed; its ruins now are part of a small park.

Seven miles upriver we come to Upper Agency State Park, where plaques show the locations of the buildings gutted by fire. Here, however, 145 Dakota families had turned to farming, and many of them helped the whites escape. Two miles south of the Upper Agency, we come to the spot where the war ended six weeks after it began, in the Battle of Wood Lake. A granite shaft names the seven soldiers who died; the Dakota casualties, which included Chief Mankato, were much heavier.

On the way downriver, we stop at Fort Ridgely, which Chief Big Eagle called "the door to the valley as far as St. Paul." It was a fort in name only: It didn't have a stockade or even a well, and it was surrounded by wooded ravines on three sides. But it had fearsome artillery, and when Big Eagle, Little Crow and Mankato attacked on the third day of the war—too late, as it turned out—the men and women inside were able to defend it for a week, until troops from Fort Snelling arrived.

Today, there's an interpretive center in the restored commissary, reconstructed foundations of the barracks and a scale model that colorfully evokes the siege.

We take picturesque County Road 21 along the river to New Ulm, stopping on the way at the Harkin Store, a general store frozen in 1870, when it was frequented by steamboats on the river across the street. There, costumed site manager Opal Dewanz shows us some of the goods, 40 percent of which are original.

"This is paregoric, the baby sitter of the day," she says. "You put a drop on a baby's tongue, and it knocked him right out," she says. "It was opium, so you had to be careful not to use too much."

New Ulm, the largest town near Dakota territory, was attacked the second day of the war by young braves who wanted to plunder it. Their detour probably saved Fort Ridgely. The city burned, but its citizens kept the Dakota at bay from a small barricade. Today, a monument in a street median marks the battles.

For the Dakota, it all ended December 26 in Mankato, where 38 warriors were hanged. The site, squeezed between railroad tracks and busy Riverfront Drive across from the regional library, is marked by a large stone buffalo. About 1,700 other Dakota people, mostly women and children, were marched upriver to Fort Snelling and imprisoned over the winter of 1862–63; hundreds died, and the rest were put on steamboats and taken to barren lands in South Dakota, where hundreds more died. A plaque tells the story.

Little Crow had been right: "If you strike at them, they will all turn on you and devour you and your women and little children . . . you will die like the rabbits when the hungry wolves hunt them in the Hard Moon."

❂ TRIP TIPS: Minnesota River Valley

• **Getting there:** By car, it's possible to see all the historic sites in two days, but three days would be ideal. For a weeklong trip, try canoeing the 60 river miles between the Upper Sioux Agency and Fort Ridgely. Call the DNR at (612) 296-6157 or (800) 766-6000 and ask for the Minnesota River No. 2 Canoe Route map.

• **Events:** Lower Sioux Pow Wow in Morton and Fort Ridgely Historic Festival, second full weekend in June, (507) 426-7888 or (507) 697-6321.

   Stone House Fourth of July, Lower Sioux Agency, (507) 697-6321, the Sunday closest to the Fourth.

   Children's Day, Lower Sioux Agency, second Saturday in August.

   Gathering of Kinship at Birch Coulee, Morton, Labor Day weekend through 1998.

   Grand Excursion, along the river from Fort Ridgely to Lower Sioux Agency Historic Site, Saturday after Labor Day. (507) 697-6321.

Traverse des Sioux Encampment, St. Peter, weekend after Labor Day. (507) 931-2160.

Mdewakanton Pow Wow, Mankato, second or third weekend in September. (800) 657-4733.

The Harkin Store holds special events in the summer, (507) 354-2016.

- **Accommodations:** The Dakota Inn in Redwood Falls, (800) 287-5443, has conventionally nice rooms, $29–$49. The city also has many chain motels.

- **Background:** *The Sioux Uprising of 1862,* by Kenneth Carley, $8.50; *Through Dakota Eyes,* narrative accounts of the war; and the young people's publications *The Dakota* and *Dakota and Ojibwe People in Minnesota* ($3.50 each) are all available from the Minnesota Historical Society, (800) 647-7827 or (612) 297-3243. KTCA's hourlong "Dakota Conflict" is available for $23.95 by calling (800) 999-0212.

- **Information:** Call the Redwood Regional tourism bureau, (800) 657-7070, for a visitors guide and a map of the Scenic Byway that includes all the historic sites. A very good map, such as a *De-Lorme Atlas & Gazetteer,* also is helpful.

Laura Ingalls Wilder Historic Highway

Pilgrims' route on the prairie

The young woman from Kyoto stood in front of the pioneer schoolhouse, shifted the toddler on her hip, faced the camera and smiled.

Snap! It's a souvenir to show friends and relatives back in Japan, where *Little House on the Prairie* is one of the most popular TV programs. The 1974–83 show is why Tadashi and Yuka Mio have come to Walnut Grove, the tiny farming town on the southwest Minnesota prairie where the show was set.

"I watch the program since I was very young," explains Yuka Mio. "I like how it shows American families relating. Especially I like Michael Landon—we think he's a typical American father, very warm-hearted and strong."

There are worse things foreign tourists could think about America. Few readers in any country are immune to the romanticism purveyed in the books written by Laura Ingalls Wilder about her childhood on the American frontier of the 1870s and 1880s.

For years, fans have found their way to the Walnut Grove farm where the Ingalls family first lived in a damp dugout with a greased-paper window. Like the Mios, many visitors even continue along Highway 14 to visit nearby Sleepy Eye—not because it has any link to Wilder, but because it was often mentioned on the TV show as the place to which Pa Ingalls took his grain to sell.

Boosters of the towns along Highway 14 couldn't help but notice these pilgrimages—occasionally, whole busloads of Japanese tourists show up—and thought: Why not hitch the whole highway to the "Little House" bandwagon? Now, brown highway signs proclaim the Laura Ingalls Wilder Historic Highway from Mankato to the South Dakota border.

Laura's prairie starts in earnest west of New Ulm. Sleepy Eye's grasp on a Wilder link is tenuous—it was only 2 years old in 1874, when the author's family moved to Walnut Grove, and its flour mill was nine years in the future. But there's still a feel of immigrant enterprise in this busy town of 3,700, many of whom gather at Schultz's Cafe for noon specials of ham or pork with sauerkraut and dumplings.

Springfield, besides having a great playground, water slide and swimming pool in Riverside Park, is giving its main street a turn-of-the-century look and has an espresso parlor, Victorian Gardens. A few miles farther, just south of Highway 14, is the Sod House on the Prairie, where replicas of an 1880 "rich man's" soddie and a poor man's dugout sit amid 10 acres of restored prairie.

"We get a lot of people on pilgrimages," says Virginia Mc-Cone, who runs the soddie year-round as a bed-and-breakfast. "People spend their whole vacation doing it. They're in love with Laura Ingalls Wilder."

For fans, mecca is Walnut Grove. Every July, when townspeople put on their elaborate "Fragments of a Dream" pageant, thousands pour into town. The Wilder Museum contains a mishmash of memorabilia that includes letters written to Wilder by schoolchildren around the world, newspaper clippings and publicity photos of the "Little House" stars but only one actual possession, a quilt made by Laura and her daughter, Rose. A self-guided tour leads visitors to the site of the dugout along Plum Creek, which washed away in the 1920s, and to the sites of the family's church and school. Take along imagination: Nothing remains except the church bell Pa helped buy with money he meant to spend on boots.

Laura's family spent only 3½ years in Walnut Grove, broken by short stints in Spring Valley, Minnesota, and Burr Oak, Iowa, before heading along what is now Highway 14 to De Smet, South Dakota, setting of *Little Town on the Prairie* and five other books.

On the way is Tyler, a town settled by Danes that maintains Danish folk traditions through an annual festival and family camps at its historic Danebod complex. It has a Danish bakery, gift shop and a B&B called Babette's Feast.

Farther on, Lake Benton sits on its 5-mile-long namesake. The 1896 Lake Benton Opera House programs concerts and plays throughout the year.

De Smet, an hour from the Minnesota border, became the home of the Ingalls family in 1879, when Laura was 12. The Laura Ingalls Wilder Memorial Society gives tours of 18 sites mentioned in the books, including the railroad surveyors' shanty where the family first lived; the frame home Pa built in 1887, which includes many family belongings; and the cemetery where Pa and Ma are buried. De Smet puts on an annual pageant named after the books, such as *By the Shores of Silver Lake,* near the site of the homestead claim outside town where the family lived for seven years.

In De Smet, the family's wanderings finally ended. But Laura's story was just beginning.

❂ TRIP TIPS: Laura Ingalls Wilder Historic Highway

- **Laura Ingalls Wilder Museum in Walnut Grove:** Open daily April through October and in winter by appointment. Admission is $1. (507) 859-2358 or (507) 859-2155.

  "Fragments of a Dream" is given the first three weekends of July. Admission is $6 general, $7 reserved. Info line: (800) 761-1009. For tickets and reservations for campsites at Plum Creek Park, call (507) 859-2174 or write Box 313T, Walnut Grove, Minnesota 56180, after Jan. 1.

- **De Smet:** The Wilder Memorial Society, (800) 880-3383 or (605) 854-3383, gives tours, $5, daily June–September; Monday–Saturday in October–December and April–May; and Monday–Friday in January–March. Its pageant is held the last weekend of June and the first two in July. Tickets are $5, $2 for children; no advance tickets are sold, but no one is turned away.
- **Accommodations:** There's one place to rent in Walnut Grove, a small, two-bedroom house called The Little House, $40–$50, (507) 859-2154. Sod House on the Prairie near Sanborn, $60–$125, (507) 723-5138. Springfield's Riverside Park has campsites, (507) 723-4416 or (507) 723-5290.

  The Wilder Memorial Society sends information about lodgings in De Smet.
- **Information:** Redwood Regional Tourism, (800) 657-7070, sends out a brochure about the towns along the highway.

Pipestone

Home of a sacred quarry

The young Cree actor from Toronto walked among the massive granite boulders called the Three Maidens, looking for something. Finally, he spotted it, a few threads of tobacco and sage tucked into a crevice.

"It gives me faith in people," he said, satisfied.

Kennetch Charlette and his sister, Valerie, had come to make the traditional offering of tobacco at the boulders before visiting the quarries at nearby Pipestone National Monument, which, according to legend, are guarded by spirits who dwell under the Three Maidens.

Cheek-by-jowl with the revered rocks were a dozen white tepees, used in the town's popular "Song of Hiawatha" pageant. But these were part of the white man's tradition and, for the visitors from Toronto, almost beneath notice. "It's just for show and money," said Valerie Charlette with a shrug.

In Pipestone, the two traditions spring from the same source: the vein of smooth, soft red rock that lies under quartzite heaved out of the southwest Minnesota prairie eons ago. For centuries, native people of many tribes visited the quarries to mine the unusual red stone, considered the flesh and blood of their ancestors, and to carve it into the ceremonial pipes whose smoke carried messages to the Great Spirit.

The quarry's fame spread to white traders and explorers. Painter George Catlin visited it in 1836 and gave pipestone its official name, catlinite. His writings about the quarry and the peace pipes made from it caught the notice of Henry Wadsworth Longfellow, who used it in his 1855 poem "Song of Hiawatha."

The hit poem, a hodgepodge of Chippewa, Iroquois and other legends mixed with overblown Victorian romanticism, immediately introduced Pipestone to tourists.

Today, the sacred quarry is a national monument visited by more than 100,000 each year and mined by people of all tribal affiliations. The "Song of Hiawatha" pageant, performed for nearly half a century, brings another 10,000 to its amphitheater in an old quartzite quarry.

The town still is lined with handsome buildings of local Sioux quartzite, including the 1888 Calumet Hotel and the 1896 Leon Moore Building, with a facade featuring a dozen sandstone gargoyles, including an ogre blowing a raspberry and a jester thumbing his nose.

On the same block is the Pipestone County Museum, its 1896 quartzite facade topped by stepped gables. Here, galleries include the accouterments of white settlers and local tribes, including items used in *Dances With Wolves,* and also of Civil War soldiers from the area.

As it was during frontier boom days, the Calumet Hotel is the anchor of downtown Pipestone. It's a lovely old building with renovated, antiques-furnished rooms that transcend the bordello-red carpet and Days Inn sign tacked onto its craggy facade.

From here, all paths lead north to Pipestone National Monument, established in 1937. But instead of heading out right away on the interpretive trail, suggests maintenance foreman Chuck Derby, a quarrier and pipemaker for more than 35 years, see the eight-minute slide show in the visitors center. Chat with a ranger. Watch the tribal artisans at work and ask them questions about the symbols used or the spiritual nature of the stone, which some American Indians feel should not be displayed or sold to tourists.

Others, like Derby, feel pipestone objects are invested with sacred meaning only when they have been blessed for ceremonial uses, and that exposure to the traditions helps white people understand and respect Indian culture.

Then, head out to the legendary source.

It's easy to see why people would see the hand of the Great Spirit at work here. Miles and miles of unbroken grass prairie—and suddenly fractured piles of red quartzite, like rock candy on a stick. The ¾-mile Circle Trail leads past small operating pits, past sumac used as pipe stems, along Pipestone Creek to Winnewissa Falls.

Around it is a lone column called Leaping Rock, to which young braves jumped to prove their valor. On ledges nearby are initials from the first official visitors, members of the 1838 Nicollet Expedition, and, on Inscription Rock, the names of pioneers a half-century later.

The trail continues through an arched stairway and above the falls, lending a view of a rugged profile jutting from the rock—the Oracle, whom tribal shamans believed could talk.

But a message already is conveyed at the monument—an ancient one of harmony with nature. And, for those who listen, it comes through loud and clear.

✪ TRIP TIPS: Pipestone

- **Pipestone National Monument:** Open 8 A.M. to 5 P.M. daily and, Memorial Day to Labor Day, to 6 p.m. Monday through Thursday and to 8 p.m. Friday through Sunday. For quiet strolls, arrive early. Admission is $2 per person or $4 for families; free for American Indians. Call (507) 825-5464.
- **Events:** Water Tower Festival, last weekend in June.
  "Song of Hiawatha," last two weekends in July and first weekend of August. For tickets, $7, call (507) 825-4126.
  Civil War Festival, third weekend in August in even-numbered years.
- **Nightlife:** Pipestone Performing Arts Center schedules many concerts and plays; call (800) 535-7610 or (507) 825-5871.
- **Accommodations:** Days Inn Historic Calumet, (800) 535-7610, has attractive rooms furnished with antiques and modern rooms, $52, and rooms with whirlpools, $90.
- **Information:** (507) 825-3316.

6 BICYCLE TRAILS

Wisconsin Bike Trails
Elroy-Sparta a famous first

The tunnel walls were moist and slimy, like the inside of a whale's belly, and the cold made the sweat on my arms clammy. The thick silence was penetrated only by dripping and our footfalls through soggy limestone.

This was Wisconsin's Elroy-Sparta bicycle trail. I'd been hearing about it for years: granddaddy of all state trails. First to use an abandoned rail bed. Three long, spooky tunnels.

For me, the thrills came on Tunnel No. 2. Large signs warned cyclists to walk their bikes through, and that's what I was doing.

But a rather large high school boy, silhouetted in the sunshine streaming in from the west end of the tunnel, wasn't. He was barreling straight toward me.

"Watch out!" I said, then stood, frozen, not understanding why he kept coming. "Heyheyheyhey!" shouted my husband. "Get off your bike! GET OFF YOUR BIKE!" Finally, a foot from my front tire, the boy veered away. I looked back and saw the same thing he had: nothing. The darkness of the tunnel had enveloped him.

And that's how I almost became road kill on the famous Elroy-Sparta.

The trail does provide a one-of-a-kind ride. Its route, though, paralleling a busy highway, no longer puts it at the top of the heap.

A lot has changed since I was a college student pounding down Iowa's back roads, marveling at the idea of a 32-mile trail just for bicycles. Wisconsin now has hundreds of miles of state touring

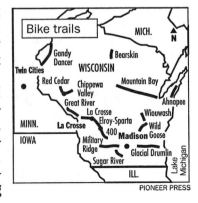

trails, mostly surfaced with finely crushed limestone, and more are being added all the time. County trails and trails for mountain bikes and ATVs expand the network even further.

Those used to paved trails may look askance at Wisconsin's finally crushed limestone. Dust gets onto gears, and the extra drag makes pulling baby carts a little harder. In spring, or after heavy rainfalls, the limestone becomes soft and mushy.

On the other hand, it keeps away roller bladers and maniacal racers, yet it's nearly as smooth as asphalt. And many people prefer its natural appearance.

Wisconsin happened onto the bicycle-trail forefront by accident in 1965, when the Chicago and North Western offered the state its Elroy-Sparta rail bed for a pittance. The state made a hiking trail out of it, but saw bicyclists using it and resurfaced it for touring. The towns along the trail promoted it, *National Geographic* and other publications wrote it up, and soon, dollars from bicycle tourism began to pour in.

The first people we met in Elroy were a couple who had driven up from Illinois. They planned to spend the better part of a week riding the three trails that radiate from the town, where the slick new Elroy Commons houses showers, shelters and an office that dispenses passes, information and rental bikes.

Wisconsin vies with Michigan for the No. 1 spot in the nation in rail-corridor miles converted to trails. Minnesota and Iowa also are in the top five. These are good times for bicycle tourists.

✿ TRIP TIPS: Wisconsin's State Trails

All trails are along abandoned rail beds and use crushed limestone except as noted. Trail passes, required for bicyclists 16 and older, cost $3 daily, $10 seasonal, include cross-country skiing in winter and can be purchased at businesses near trails, self-registration boxes or by calling (608) 266-2181. Facilities close for the winter at the end of October. For the two-map Wisconsin Bicycle Map, individual trail maps and lodging information, call (800) 432-TRIP. For information on mountain-bike and ATV trails, ask for the Summer Recreation Guide at the same number.

• **Ahnapee:** 18 miles between Algoma and Sturgeon Bay past forest, farms and swamps. (414) 487-2041, (414) 487-3214; Door County tourism, (800) 527-3529.

- **Bearskin:** 18 miles south of Minocqua through wilderness and past lakes. Compacted granite. (715) 362-7616.
- **Chippewa River:** 20 miles west of Eau Claire; the first five miles are paved. The trail links with the Red Cedar at the Chippewa River. (715) 839-1607.
- **Elroy-Sparta:** 32 miles on a rail bed between Elroy and Sparta, paralleling Highway 71. Shuttle service out of Kendall. (608) 463-7109.
- **400:** 22 miles between Elroy and Reedsburg along the Baraboo River. (608) 275-3214.
- **Gandy Dancer:** 50 miles between St. Croix Falls and Danbury. Never far from Wisconsin 35, but passes lakes and nine villages. (800) 222-7655.
- **Glacial Drumlin:** 47 miles through farmland from Cottage Grove, just east of Madison, to Waukesha, just west of Milwaukee. (414) 646-3025.
- **Great River:** 24 miles between a wildlife refuge north of Trempealeau to Onalaska through Mississippi wetlands. (800) 873-1901.
- **La Crosse:** 21.5 miles between Onalaska and Sparta, paralleling I-90. (800) 873-1901.
- **Military Ridge:** 39.6 miles between Dodgeville and Fitchburg; the 21 miles between Barneveld and Verona are the most scenic. (608) 935-5119.
- **Mountain Bay:** 80 miles between Wausau and Green Bay, rolling farmland and meadows over trout streams and past Amish farms. (800) 235-8528, (715) 524-5165.
- **Red Cedar:** 14.5 miles between Menomonie and the Chippewa River, along the Red Cedar River. Links with the Chippewa River Trail. (715) 232-2631.
- **Sugar River:** 23.5 miles along the Sugar River between picturesque New Glarus and Brodhead. Shuttle service out of New Glarus. (608) 527-2334.
- **Wild Goose:** 34 miles south of Fond du Lac, skirting the western edge of Horicon Marsh. (414) 386-3705.
- **Wiouwash:** 20 miles from Oshkosh through woodlands and meadows north to Hortonville. (414) 734-3358.

Minnesota Bike Trails
Reaping the rewards of asphalt

Mud-spattered bicyclists hoisted Cokes. A Dixieland band played. Dignitaries patted each other on the back and gave out door prizes to a crowd of hundreds milling around a little brick depot.

Elysian, Minnesota, was as blissed-out as its name, and it was all because of an 8-foot strip of asphalt.

The 39-mile Sakatah Singing Hills State Trail had just been paved, transforming it from a dusty strip of rough limestone to—local businesspeople hope—a street paved with some of the gold that the popular Root River trail has brought to Lanesboro and the other towns along it.

"Lanesboro is wonderful, I love that trail, but that's all you ever read about," says Adele Grefsrud, an avid bicyclist who owns Pit Stop 60 in Elysian. "People who live in the metro also like to come down to our cornfields, lakes and the state park."

In 1995, the Minnesota DNR finished 95 miles of new trails and paved the Sakatah (pronounced sah-KAH-tah) trail between Faribault and Mankato. It came just in time to maintain Minnesota's place as No. 3 in the nation in rail-corridor miles converted to trails, after Wisconsin and Michigan.

Why is that important? Because weekend tourists love bicycle trails, especially the asphalt ones of Minnesota.

"There's an almost insatiable appetite for these," says Dan Collins of the Minnesota DNR. "As soon as we announce a new one, people are chasing the grader down the road."

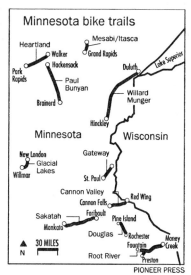

PIONEER PRESS

☺ TRIP TIPS: Minnesota bike trails

- **Cannon Valley:** 20 miles between Cannon Falls and Red Wing. Beautiful, shady ride along the Cannon River with a picnic area and ice-cream store in Welch, its midpoint. Cannon Falls is only an hour from the Twin Cities, so the trail can be crowded on weekends. Maintained by a trail association; daily fee is $2. (507) 263-3954.

- **Douglas:** 12½ miles between Pine Island's city park and outskirts of Rochester. Pleasant ride through rolling farmland, with a snack stop in Douglas. (507) 285-7176.

- **Glacial Lakes:** 12 miles between the Civic Center at the northeast edge of Willmar and New London. It goes past Spicer, worth a stop for the excellent beach on Green Lake and adjoining Melvin's restaurant. Another six miles of compacted granite continue from New London to Hawick. (612) 354-4940.

- **Heartland:** 28 miles between the lake-resort towns of Park Rapids and Walker. Pleasant ride with many small towns to explore: Akeley, home of a giant Paul Bunyan on whose outstretched hand people pose for pictures; Nevis, home of a giant muskie; and Dorset, an odd little oasis that has as many restaurants (Compadres is most popular) as houses. Visit on the first Sunday of August during Taste of Dorset, when restaurants sell samples and also votes for mayor (one year, the mayor was a 5-year-old from Chicago). The nine-mile stretch between Akeley and Walker is most scenic. (218) 652-4054.

- **Mesabi/Itasca:** The six-mile Itasca County Bike Trail north from Grand Rapids' fairgrounds shares its beginning with the first part of the planned 132-mile Mesabi Trail to Ely. Grand Rapids tourism, (800) 472-6366.

- **Paul Bunyan:** 48 miles between the western edge of Brainerd (trailhead is at Northland Arboretum, about a mile east of Highway 371's intersection with Excelsior Road) and Hackensack. Eventually, the trail will stretch 100 miles, to Bemidji. (218) 828-6081.

- **Root River:** 36 miles along the Root River between Fountain and Vinegar Ridge Recreation Area, with 48 wooden bridges. This Champs Elysees of trails, formerly a rail bed for trains ferrying logs out of Lanesboro, attracts swarms of tourists. Most people gravitate to Lanesboro, a town of century-old storefronts hugged on three sides by hills. To the east, the shaded trail winds through the picturesque hamlet of Whalan to quiet Peterson, busy Rushford and beyond eventually to Houston. To the west, the trail rolls up a slight grade to Fountain; at the midpoint, a six-mile spur leads to Preston. From there, an extension to Harmony is under way. (507) 467-2552; Lanesboro tourism, (800) 944-2670.

- **Sakatah:** 39 miles between Faribault and Mankato. From Mankato, the trail is away from the highway but on open fields; the 21½ miles between Faribault and Elysian are shadiest and most scenic. The eastern trailhead starts at the Highway 60 exit of I-35 and skirts several lakes before it reaches wooded Sakatah Lake State Park, which has trails, picnic areas and a beach. The lakes are shallow; in late summer, they tend to be full of algae that makes swimming unpleasant. Beyond the park are the pleasant towns of Waterville and Elysian; ride across the highway to see the enormous flock of pelicans that lives on Lake Elysian. (800) 507-7787.

- **Willard Munger:** There are four stretches of this trail that will link St. Paul and Duluth. For details, call (612) 296-6157 or, within Minnesota, (800) 766-6000.

  The Gateway starts on Arlington Avenue just east of I-35E in St. Paul and stretches to Pine Point Park in Stillwater Township. Many people park in a lot near Minnesota 36 and Hadley Avenue in Oakdale, where the trail parallels 36 before it heads into the country.

  The 36½-mile stretch between Hinckley and Barnum, known as the Hinckley Fire Trail, uses a rail corridor that was the scene of a dramatic rescue in 1894, when a cyclone of fire destroyed six towns, including Hinckley, where the Fire Museum holds fascinating exhibits about the fire. The 22 miles to the pretty town of Willow River is most scenic.

  The 17-mile stretch goes from Barnum to Carlton.

  The last 14½ miles from Barnum to Duluth is lovely, passing Jay Cooke State Park and the St. Louis River on a downhill grade before coming out near the Lake Superior Zoo. (612) 296-6157.

- **Information:** To get free individual maps of the state trails and the Cannon Valley Trail, call (612) 296-6157 or, within Minnesota, (800) 766-6000.

Iowa Bike Trails

"2,000 miles by 2000"

In 1988, Iowa's bicyclists hit the jackpot.
Their prize was $1 million a year, paid out in the form of asphalt or crushed-limestone trails on abandoned rail beds throughout the countryside.

Iowa pioneered across-the-state bicycle rides with the popular RAGBRAI in 1973, but it didn't get serious about trails until 1987, when the legislature looked around and saw the handsome benefits its neighbors were reaping from bicycle tourism. Once the state got started—its motto is "2,000 miles by the year 2000"—it piled on the miles.

"Actually, we're planning for 3,000 miles," says trails coordinator Nancy Burns. "Then we won't have any more abandoned rail beds, and we'll have to look elsewhere."

Iowa now is in the top five in the nation in rail-corridor miles converted to trails, according to the national Rails to Trails Conservancy.

Some of Iowa's trails are short, like the 2.3-mile Puddle Jumper, which connects the towns of Orange City, known for its Tulip Festival, and Alton. But others cruise for miles, often alongside rivers and through interesting small towns.

One of the most popular, Burns says, is the 34-mile, asphalt Raccoon River Valley Trail, west of Des Moines. It winds through a river greenbelt to the town of Adel, where bicyclists now can drink Rail Trail Ale on the patio of an adjacent brew pub. Each year, says administrator Jim Sanders, the trail brings 60,000 people into town, and the city is working on a tour of historic sites that will bring bicyclists onto its 40 blocks of brick streets to see, among other things, storefronts filmed for *The Bridges of Madison County.*

I tried one of Iowa's first trails, the 26-mile Heritage

PIONEER PRESS

Trail near Dubuque. Starting just a few miles from the Mississippi River, I rode through limestone-pocked hills along the placid Little Maquoketa River, past Sundown Ski Area and then pastures.

It was Friday afternoon, but the trail was quiet, with just as many walkers as bikers. In tiny Graf, it left the river valley and emerged into hilly farmland. I turned back, but the next day picked the trail up at its western trailhead, the busy farming town of Dyersville. There, I looked doubtfully at the trail, stretching off into the afternoon haze, and consulted a woman from Milwaukee who had just ridden 10 miles out and back.

"It was pretty desolate," she said. "I thought it would be hilly, but it was flat, all plains and fields."

I put my bike back on the car and went, instead, to see the *Field of Dreams* movie site, three miles northeast of town. It was early May, and the corn hadn't even sprouted, but cars from five states were parked in a lot next to the diamond, their occupants emerging with two items: baseball gloves and video cameras.

Not all Iowa bike trails have connections to movies, though the River City Trail links Clear Lake, where Buddy Holly played the night he died in a plane crash, and Mason City, setting for *The Music Man*. For five miles, the 15½-mile trail parallels an electric trolley, still in service.

Many of these trails are more interesting than Iowa-bashers would think. Even so, it pays to look closely at the state's excellent trails guide. As elsewhere, trails that parallel rivers generally are scenic, and those that parallel highways aren't.

After all, this state doesn't claim to be heaven—just Iowa.

☺ TRIP TIPS: Iowa bike trails

- **Heritage Trail:** 26 miles of crushed limestone between Dyersville and Sageville, just north of Dubuque. Daily fee: $1.10. There are many historic inns in Dubuque; call (800) 255-2255. Dyersville has several chain motels; call (319) 875-2311.

- **Raccoon River Valley Trail:** 34 miles of asphalt, starting in Waukee, 10 miles west of Des Moines. Daily fee: $1. For tourist information, call the Adel chamber, (515) 993-4525.

- **Cedar Valley Trail:** 52 miles of crushed limestone from Evansdale, just south of Waterloo, to Hiawatha, north of Cedar Rapids.

La Porte City, 15 miles south of Evansdale, would make a good overnight. For a brochure, call the Black Hawk County Conservation Board at (319) 266-0328.

- **Dickinson County Spine Trail:** 12 miles of asphalt through the tourist areas of Lake Okoboji, Arnolds Park and Spirit Lake. Call (800) 839-9987 for tourist information.

- **Great River Road Trail:** 16 miles of concrete following a county road along river from McGregor to Guttenberg. Very scenic and very steep. Call the McGregor chamber, (319) 873-2186.

- **Prairie Farmer Recreational Trail:** 18 miles of crushed limestone through native prairie between Calmar and Cresco. Call Winneshiek County/Decorah tourism, (319) 382-3990.

- **River City Trail:** 15½ miles of asphalt, crushed limestone and city streets between Clear Lake and Mason City. Call Clear Lake tourism, (515) 357-2159.

- **Three Rivers Trail:** 36½ miles of crushed limestone, including 36 railway bridges, between Rolfe and Eagle Grove. Call the Humboldt chamber, (515) 332-1481.

- **Information:** For a detailed guide to Iowa's trails and nearby facilities and attractions, send $7.50 to Iowa Natural Heritage Foundation, 505 Fifth Ave., Suite 444, Des Moines, Iowa 50309-2321; call (515) 288-1846 with questions.

7 NORTHWOODS WISCONSIN

Bayfield
Crossroads on Chequamegon Bay

In Bayfield, Wisconsin, all kinds of paths cross.
Three hundred years ago, Hurons and Ottawas trickled in from the east, driven out by the Iroquois. French explorers and fur traders paddled in across Lake Superior, and many other tribes—Fox, Potawatomi, Menominee, the local Ojibwe—converged on their posts to sell them pelts. Priests crisscrossed Chequamegon Bay, intent on converting the Indians.

The fur trade fizzled out, and in 1854, the Indians began moving to reservations. Bayfield became a town and speculators poured in, each dreaming of fortunes. Sawmills ate up the pine forests and shipped out the lumber, turning Chequamegon Bay into a big mill pond. Quarries sent brownstone to Chicago and Milwaukee; fisheries packed off herring and whitefish to points east.

Things had calmed down considerably by the 1920s, by which time it was obvious Bayfield would not be the next Chicago or St. Paul. Orchards took the place of the pine forests. Today, Bayfield's natural resources are different, but still abundant: fields of pink and blue lupines in late spring, strawberries and raspberries in summer, pears and apples in fall and herring whenever it decides to run.

Tourists, especially those suffering from hay fever, have been making their way to Bayfield virtually since its birth. They still are converging on the town from all points. From it, many kayak to the remoter Apostle Islands or take the ferry to Madeline Island; in winter, they ski down nearby Mount Ashwabay or out to the ice caves at Squaw Bay.

Weekenders stay in Queen Anne showplaces built by the first millionaires, eat whitefish still caught daily and, like their forebears, stroll around this quiet hillside village with the great views.

Late afternoon is a good time to arrive in Bayfield. The slanting rays of sun glance off the white hulls of sailboats bobbing in the harbor and the flapping sails of the Zeeto, a three-masted reproduction of an 1870 fishing schooner that is returning from its afternoon cruise. Sunburned sailors climb off their boats, and the Madeline Island ferry pulls up to the dock, disgorging bicyclists, pedestrians and a long line of cars.

I have two evenings in Bayfield, sandwiched around a sea-kayaking trip; I check the ferry schedule and head for Maggie's on Manypenny Avenue. It's only 5:30 P.M. on a Monday, but Maggie's, where the locals hang out, is almost full. I find my favorite beer from Oregon on the beer list and contemplate the specials—pan-roasted pheasant, grilled rack of lamb, grilled duck sausage—but settle on the fajitas.

The food is serious here, but the attitude isn't: Retro prints of flamingos line the walls and, hanging from the ceiling, are a tassled pink pinata and strings of red-chili and flamingo lights. After I finish my heaping plate of garlicky beef and sauteed peppers, I walk past the shops of Rittenhouse Avenue to the harbor.

I have no real reason to visit Madeline Island, but it's a wonderful evening to be on the water. I walk onto the ferry, and 20 minutes later I'm walking down La Pointe's Main Street, which is modest, and around the Yacht Club, which isn't. It's full of fancy yachts, including one that should be dubbed *Greek Tycoon* rather than *Northlander*.

On the other side of the marina is a little Ojibwe burial ground, where fur trader Michel Cadotte and his Ojibwe wife, born Equaysayway but baptised Madeline, are buried. In one leafy niche, tributes have been left for the revered Chief Buffalo—bead earrings, coins, feathers, small baskets. Shin-high frame "houses" cover other graves, sheltering their inhabitants and the food needed on the journey to the afterlife.

When the ferry deposits me back in Bayfield, the sun is down and the busiest spot in town is the ice-cream hut next to Greunke's, known for its old-fashioned fish boils.

My next evening I head back to Maggie's, where I again fail to try the town specialty, though buttons sold at local stores read "Real tourists eat whitefish livers." Afterward, I cross the street, slip between piles of lumber and am on a trail a local shopkeeper told me about, an abandoned rail corridor that heads south down the Bayfield peninsula. Through a frame of trees, I walk and look down at sailboats gliding between Madeline and the mainland.

In early October, a crowd of up to 50,000 descends on this town of 685 for Apple Fest, but after that, locals take a breather, says Mayor Larry MacDonald, and about half of the shops close for winter. MacDonald, who once owned a ski resort, likes the cold weather. Like many residents of Bayfield, he and his wife, Julie, once lived in the Twin Cities. They bought the Cooper Hill House B&B but kept an office in the Cities for two years, until they couldn't bear to leave Bayfield at all.

"It was either a perfect day for sailing or a perfect day for skiing," MacDonald says. So he sold his manufacturer's-rep agency and bought the Apostle Islands Outfitters and General Store.

"The trick is, everybody up here has two or three things going to support themselves," he says, but it's worth it: "Bayfield is the best place in the world."

✪ TRIP TIPS: Bayfield

- **Events:** Race Week, last week of June.
  Red Cliff Powwow, Fourth of July weekend.
  Festival of Arts, last weekend in July.
  Schooner Races, weekend before Apple Fest.
  Apple Fest, first full weekend in October.
  Run on Water to Madeline Island, second Sunday in February.
  Blue Moon Ball, third Saturday in February.
- **Tours:** Ferries to Madeline Island run until the bay freezes. Cost is $3 each way for those 12 and over, $1.75 for those 6–11. Cars cost $5.75 until Oct. 15, then $4.75 until May 15. (715) 747-2051 or (715) 747-6801.
  The Apostle Islands Cruise Service runs a three-hour narrated Grand Tour of the Apostles daily from late May to mid-October, $22. The Zeeto makes 3½-hour cruises daily from Memorial Day through mid-September, $45. Camper shuttles and special cruises also are offered. (800) 323-7619, (715) 779-3925.
  Trek & Trail, (800) 354-8735, offers dog-sledding and ski trips in winter and kayaking trips to the Apostles in summer.
- **Accommodations:** Book early for summer and fall weekends. Highest rates are for summer.
  Nearest the harbor are Bayfield Inn, (715) 779-3363, $45–$85, on the park; Bay Front Inn, (715) 779-3330, $55–$125, with

balconies; and the old-fashioned Greunke's, (800) 245-3072, $45–$85, known for its fish boils.

The posh Old Rittenhouse Inn, (715) 779-5111, $99–$199, is very popular; book rooms early. The Cooper Hill House, (715) 779-5060, $67–$88, is among the many other B&Bs.

- **Dining:** Maggie's, the Rittenhouse and the Clubhouse on Madeline Island (May–October) serve very good food.
- **Apostle Islands National Lakeshore Visitor Center:** Campers can pick up free permits at the center in Bayfield's old county courthouse at Washington Avenue and Fourth Street. There's a free movie and exhibits. Open daily Memorial Day through October and weekdays in winter. (715) 779-3397.
- **Information:** Bayfield Chamber of Commerce, (800) 447-4094.

Big Top Chautauqua

Music and laughter under the big tent

As darkness falls around the big blue-and-white tent, the curtains part.

With one set of musicians on one side of the stage, singers and actors on the other and a big screen showing old photographs in the middle, Bayfield's past unfolds in "Riding the Wind," with more memorable, foot-tapping songs than a Broadway musical.

In 1856, Bayfield is being hyped as "a new Chicago! Bigger than St. Paul!" Fur traders make an appearance—"they had to carry a tune as well as a pack"—and the musicians sing a rousing voyageurs' song in French. Ojibwe Gerry DePerry tells how the Apostle Islands were created—the great Wenabojoo, angry at a beaver, threw rocks into Lake Superior, forming the islands.

Some of the characters are famous ones—Radisson and Groseilliers, known locally as "Radishes and Gooseberries," whose 1660 exploration of the Lake Superior's southern shore and other areas led to the founding of the Hudson Bay Co.— and some aren't: the late Ray Cahill, longtime town barber, who arrived in a covered wagon in 1924.

It's a heck of a history lesson, and it's the flagship show of Bayfield's Big Top Chautauqua on a ski hill outside town.

Other revues—"Keeper of the Light," based on journals kept by Apostle Islands lighthouse keepers, and "On the Velvet," about old-time railroad life—also have become crowd pleasers, but they're only part of the summerlong season. In addition to many regional performers, Arlo Guthrie, Emily Lou Harris, Leo Kottke and Leon Redbone also have performed under the 750-seat tent, which has the intimate feel of a nightclub.

✪ TRIP TIPS: Big Top Chautauqua in Bayfield

- **When:** Early June through Labor Day weekend.
- **Tickets:** Reserved seats are $16 for adults, $8 for children 12 and under. Open seating is $10 for adults, $3 for children. For tickets, call (715) 373-5552.
- **Dining:** Fish-boil dinners—fresh whitefish from Lake Superior with new potatoes and coleslaw—are offered on the Big Top site every Friday night for $7. On Saturday nights, barbecued ribs and chicken are offered for $7. There's a bar next door.

Waterfalls
Roaring remnants of the Ice Age

I'd never really grasped the Ice Age until I stood at the head of Big Manitou Falls, 15 miles south of Superior, Wisconsin.

Below me was a wild and rocky gorge, eventually vanishing beneath a lumpy carpet of treetops that stretches to Lake Superior, once glacial Lake Duluth.

The falls at Pattison State Park are spectacular; with a 165-foot drop, they're the highest in Wisconsin and the fourth-highest east of the Rockies. But the panorama north is nearly as arresting; I could almost see that big glacier sitting on the horizon, starting to melt and make geologic history.

The northwest corner of Wisconsin is waterfall country. Over the last billion years, geologic forces have created hun-

dreds of waterfalls, some roaring torrents, others delicate trick-
les hidden away in state forests. Douglas, Bayfield, Ashland
and Iron counties, the four counties that border on Superior's
South Shore, contain the state's nine largest falls.

In every season, they are striking. In fall, their banks are
crowded with red, orange and yellow foliage; in winter, their
cascades turn crystalline; in spring, tons of thundering rain-
water make rock walls vibrate.

For Big Manitou, as for other waterfalls, it all began when
ancient flows of lava welled from splits in the Earth's crust.
Later, this layer was covered by softer sandstone deposited at
the bottom of the ocean that once covered the area. Subse-
quent movement within the Earth created faults that pushed
the volcanic rock nearer the surface, and when rivers created
by glacial meltwater began to cut valleys and gorges through
the sandstone, that harder rock refused to erode. And it's holding up the waterfalls today.

At Pattison State Park, a second falls was cut by the Black
River. A mile upstream along hiking trails is Little Manitou Falls,
which drops 31 feet in a cozy forest setting. Between is Inter-
falls Lake, with a curving, red-sand beach that becomes busy
in summer.

At Amnicon Falls State Park, 17 miles to the east, the sound
of rushing water is everywhere. The Amnicon River splits around
an island covered with skinny red pines and cedar and creates
a whole series of falls, which can be seen from a circling trail.

A covered bridge divides Upper and Lower falls, where the
red rock of the bank has worn away in a curious rippling pat-
tern. Across the island is Snakepit Falls and a falls that gurgles
through a gate made of boulders. Picnic tables and grills line
the river.

Fifty miles farther east is Ashland, a good base for waterfall
explorations. Ashland, south of the Apostle Islands on Chequamegon Bay, once was a busy port and rail town.

It's not so busy anymore, which makes the existence of the
Hotel Chequamegon a surprise. The handsome, three-story
white hotel overlooking the bay, with two corner turrets and a
multilevel roof, comes from the tradition of Victorian grand hotels but was built in 1986, on the site of a 19th century original
that twice was destroyed by fire.

Inside, the hotel is filled with gorgeous hardwood trim, antiques, lace and fireplaces; rooms have high ceilings. There's a small pool on the lower level and two restaurants.

Seventeen miles south of Ashland is Copper Falls State Park, home of the eighth- and ninth-highest falls. This is a beautiful park in itself, wild like the great national parks of the West. Its deep canyon was cut by the Bad River, and its rapids are frequented by fly fishermen.

A fenced forest path, some of it handicapped-accessible, skirts the rim of the gorge through white cedars. At Copper Falls, the horehound-colored waters of the Bad River plunge 30 feet in twin torrents. They join another river at Brownstone Falls, where Tyler's Fork Creek plunges 30 feet over a black-lava bed into the Bad River's gorge. Sometimes, when the light is right, its spray creates a rainbow.

The two rivers then surge across the narrow waist of Devil's Gate, where a buttress of "peanut-brittle" rock juts over the river—a slab of rock studded with rounded boulders, up-ended by the Earth's heavings. Copper was mined here, by ancient inhabitants as well as 19th century enterpreneurs, but the veins are thin.

Next door in Iron County, which borders Michigan's Upper Peninsula, are another 11 waterfalls, seven of them along the Montreal River. In Wisconsin, the Ice Age left plenty of mementos.

❂ TRIP TIPS: Wisconsin's Waterfalls

- **Maps:** Wisconsin's Summer Recreation Guide lists the falls and gives locations. Call (800) 432-TRIP for a free copy.
- **Accommodations:** Hotel Chequamegon (pronounced sha-WAH-megun), (800) 946-5555, has rooms or suites with kitchenettes, $50–$140.

     Pattison, Amnicon and Copper Falls state parks have campsites; Pattison and Copper Falls have a few set up for winter camping.
- **Fees:** Daily state-park admission is $4 for residents, $6 for non-residents, $2 for a one-hour pass. Several parks can be visited on one daily pass.
- **Information:** Ashland Area Chamber of Commerce, (715) 682-2500; Pattison and Amnicon state parks, (715) 399-8073; Copper Falls, (715) 274-5123.

Historic Lodges
A checkered but romantic past

In the early part of this century, Chicago was not always a pleasant place to live. It was rough, dirty and already known as "the wickedest city in the United States" when Prohibition flung open the door to organized crime.

Those who could afford to leave for the summer did. Many headed for the lakes of northwest Wisconsin, a two-day trip from the city.

Wealthy businessman Jacob Loeb came because he needed a vacation from notoriety. He bought land on remote Lake Namekagon near Cable after his teen-age nephew, Richard Loeb, was convicted with friend Nathan Leopold of murdering a young boy for the thrill of it.

The 1924 trial was sensational, and the boy's father died that year of a heart attack. His uncle paid the celebrated lawyer Clarence Darrow a king's ransom to defend him—and save him from the electric chair, which he did.

Ted Moody came for the fresh air, his lungs having been poisoned by fumes in the garage he operated. Al Capone came for a break from the considerable health risks of his business, racketeering.

Multimillionaire Frank Stout came for privacy and got it on his Island of Happy Days. Grain broker Charles Lewis came for the fly fishing and then bought the tract of virgin white pine his stream was on, thus saving it from the saws of logging barons like Frank Stout.

These men built retreats now open to the public, marvelous old lodges with massive log beams, fieldstone fireplaces and stuffed bobcats and bears snarling in corners. To create such a lodge today would be impossible: For one thing, nothing can duplicate the smell of old pine or cedar, rubbed into a dark glossiness over the decades. For another thing, these retreats all have a history. Like the logs, they have acquired a certain patina with the passage of time.

Garmisch USA, named for the Bavarian town where the 1936 Winter Olympics were held, is only eight miles down the road from Telemark ski resort—also inspired by Garmisch, where its founder, the late Tony Wise, was stationed as a GI in postwar Germany.

The Germanic romanticism of Garmisch USA, however, is borrowed not from the slopes but from the medieval hunting lodge, which melds well with northwoods rusticity. An iron chandelier hangs in the two-story great room, along with strings of muskies, stuffed foxes, stags, bobcats and ducks.

My large room has a miniature suit of armor set into its padded door, and its decor is in some nether zone between the 1920s and '90s, but it has a wood-burning stove and 25 feet of picture window, which give me a drop-dead view of the pink-streaked sunset over Lake Namekagon.

I have dinner in the wood-paneled restaurant and stroll around the grounds. This was the retreat of Jacob Loeb, son of poor German Jews whose first job was selling dry goods in the basement of a Chicago department store. He was an early investor in Sears Roebuck but was dedicated to the poor, leading United Drives in 1922 and 1925 that raised $6.5 million.

He died in 1944, and in 1955 the land and buildings were sold to Jean Funk, a young skier from an affluent Chicago family. She renamed it Garmisch USA and gave it a Bavarian look. Today, the Cable resort is owned and run by a couple from North Dakota, Bruce and Shelby Niebergall.

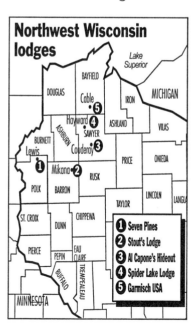

Not far south, at Spider Lake Lodge near Hayward, Paul Grossi slides a video-tape into the VCR. It shows jerky footage from the 1920s: Ted Moody hewing logs for the lodge, and Hank Smith, a local Chippewa, laboriously shaping the wood chinking between them that still looks so handsome today.

Moody wasn't a rich man,

says Grossi. He and Smith built the lodge and cabins, now privately owned, and Moody and his family ran them as a resort.

Today, the lodge, now a B&B, is little changed; rows of the original paned windows stretch along the dining-room walls, overlooking the lake, and polished maple floors stretch into a screened porch and common room, where Adirondack rockers sit next to stitched-parchment lamps. Smallish rooms have the feel of a cabin.

"One of my guests said once, 'It's a typical north Wisconsin lodge like when I was little, except you can't find them anymore,'" Grossi says.

Over a few county roads to the south, near Couderay, is a very untypical retreat, one that still has a machine-gun turret and eight-car garage, now a restaurant. It was built by Al Capone on 400 acres of logged-out land, meaning he could see his enemies coming from a long way off.

The 1925 stone-and-log house overlooks Cranberry Lake—Capone liked to fish, though the lake also was used by hydroplanes flying whiskey in from Canada. It was built for a wary comfort—two mahogany spiral staircases lead to corner bedrooms along walkways that have a full view of the living room; in Capone's room, a switch worked all the yard lights. Ceiling light fixtures are made from the hooved forelegs of deer.

J. Houston, whose family has owned Capone's estate since 1958 and runs tours of it, shows me around. She takes a fairly charitable view of the man who, it is said, ordered the murders of more than 500 people.

"He sent a lot of young people to college and opened a soup kitchen," she says. "I've had people toast his picture on the wall and say, 'Here's to you, Al, you fed me and my family when we were starving.' We've had a lot of that over the years."

Capone's vacations were peaceful, but he wouldn't have had to worry about approaching rivals if he'd had a moat, the way Frank Stout did. Stout, son of the man whose timber company became the largest in the world, built a hilltop summer estate on an island in Red Cedar Lake, near Mikana.

Stout was not known as a philanthropist like his brother, James, who endowed the institute that became the University of Wisconsin-Stout in Menomonie. But he plowed $1.5 million in 1915 money into his compound, which includes what may be the oldest bowling alley in Wisconsin.

When Stout died in 1927, his obituary listed him as one of the 10 richest men in Chicago. His widow continued to use the estate until she died there in 1949, by which time the number of tycoons who would want such a place had dwindled. The 35,000-square-foot complex had deteriorated when it was bought by a Wayzata real-estate developer and an Eau Claire ophthalmologist and opened to overnight guests in 1992.

Today, the spirit of a bygone gentility is strong. A clipped lawn, stretching down to the lake, begs for croquet players in whites. In the Great Room, classical music plays as women play cards near a crackling fire and grand piano. A small bridge leads past clumps of bluebells and jack-in-the-pulpit to another island, traversed by a pine-needle-strewn path.

The lodge, though it is built of logs, is of the north woods in spirit only: The huge beams of the dining room contain ornate Bavarian carvings of pelicans and oak leaves, the entry has Gothic arches, and the Norwegian builder has left dragon's heads on all the downspouts.

An hour west, over farmland and scrub forest that once was thick with white pines, is a place that also is on the National Register and was built the same year Stout's was started, 1903. Yet it's much different in spirit. Millionaire grain broker Charles Lewis had leased a tract of land near Lewis that included a spring-fed trout stream. When logging came uncomfortably near, he bought the land and built a lodge, naming it Seven Pines for its largest trees.

He entertained prominent sportsmen of the day, including Calvin Coolidge when he was president. After Lewis died in 1932, most of the property was logged off. Even so, the six acres around the lodge, now open to overnight guests, diners and fly fishermen, still hold virgin timber, some of which may be 300 years old.

Not much has changed, except all fishing on the private stream is catch-and-release. I arrive just before twilight, when only a few of the sun's rays penetrate the pine canopy and the only sounds are of the wind murmuring through branches and water rushing over boulders.

In the lodge, members of a fishing seminar stand in front of the fire, their cheeks ruddy with wine and the memory of dozens of trout caught. Then, on porch tables decorated with trillium bouquets, chef Ann Ward serves a simple but suave three-course meal that includes a perfectly cooked rainbow trout with a vegetable strudel.

Even Calvin Coolidge would have been impressed.

☉ TRIP TIPS: Historic Wisconsin lodges

- **Garmisch USA, 10 miles east of Cable:** Seven inn rooms are $55–$75; a suite is $125. Rates at guest homes range from $275 for two nights in the two-bedroom, two-bath Geneva to $975 for a week at the five-bedroom, five-bath Blarney Castle. Restaurant and bar are open to the public. Call (800) 794-2204 or (715) 794-2204.

- **Spider Lake Lodge B&B, 17 miles east of Hayward:** Seven rooms, $65–$90. Call (715) 462-3793 or (800) 653-9472.

- **Al Capone's Hideout, six miles north of Couderay:** Afternoon tours are $5.75 adults, $2.50 children 6–11, and are given Fridays–Sundays from Mother's Day, daily from Memorial Day through the third weekend of September, then Friday–Sunday through October. The restaurant, bar and shop are open Friday–Sunday through February and daily between Christmas and New Year's. Call (715) 945-2746.

- **Stout's Lodge, one mile north of Mikana, on an island in Red Cedar Lake:** The 32 rooms, not all with private bath, range from $88 to $159, including a continental breakfast; with all meals, rates are $165–$235, double occupancy, in high season, $125–$184 in May, October and weekdays in June and September. There's a two-night minimum for Fridays and Saturdays. Dinner, $15–$24, and Sunday brunch are open to the public. Call (715) 354-3646.

- **Seven Pines, two miles east of Lewis:** Thirteen rooms, not all with private bath, $84–$134; the Carriage House, $84–$94; Gate House, $160, and the Stream House, $180. Dinner, $24–$48, is reservations-only. Breakfast and lunch also are served. Call (715) 653-2323.

Hayward
Prize muskies and ski legends

If you wonder who rules the roost in Hayward, finish line of North America's most famous Nordic-skiing race, take a look at the water tower of the town of 2,000.

It doesn't say "Home of the Birkebeiner." It says "Home of World Record Muskies." And whose name is better-known, Manfred Nagl or Cal Johnson? Not Nagl, the Austrian racer who won the Birkie in 1990, '91 and '93.

No, more likely it's the vacationer who, way back in 1949, wrestled a world-record muskie out of the nearby Chippewa Flowage, Wisconsin's largest wilderness lake. Cal Johnson's fame is forever enshrined, along with his 67½-pound fish, at the Moccasin Bar in downtown Hayward.

And yet it's the Birkebeiner that has put Hayward on the world map. Many foreign accents are heard on Hayward's streets during the February festivities and the race itself, often won by Czech, Swiss or Austrian racers. Each year, the town hosts 20,000 to 30,000 race fans, about 10,000 of whom will ski in the 52-kilometer Birkie, the 25-kilometer Kortelopet and the children's Barnebirkie.

"Everyone who skis cross-country has heard of the Birke-beiner," says Mary Gervais, who once owned a B&B in town. "It's a little backwoodsy community, and yet they're doing some awfully big sporting events."

The Chequamegon Fat Tire Festival in September also is the largest of its kind; in the top event, 2,500 mountain-bikers bump over a 40-mile course that includes parts of the Birkie.

It all started with the late Tony Wise, a Hayward native who built Telemark on a hill near Cable in 1947 and, by 1972, had concluded that cross-country skiing was the coming thing. He built trails at Telemark and, to publicize them, decided to stage a marathon over some logging roads and county land be-tween Hayward and Cable. "I was a great believer in com-memorating every new thing I did with a big event," said Wise, shortly before his death in 1995 at 74.

He named the marathon for one in his grandmother's homeland: the Birkebeiner in Lillehammer, Norway, itself a commemoration. During a civil war in 1206, warriors rescued the infant grandson of the late King Sverre from enemy territory, skiing 55 kilometers to safety. The warriors were members of a political faction called Birkebeiners, named because they once were so poor they tied pieces of birch bark around their legs when their trousers were worn out.

Today, competitors in the race between Lillehammer and Rena still ski with a pack that weighs 12 pounds, like the little prince, who became King Haakon IV.

Only 53 people showed up for Wise's race in 1973, but the American Birkebeiner grew every year. Eventually, the rolling course was widened to 30 feet, a kind of skier's superhighway.

In 1985, Wise—whom Fat Tire organizer Gary Crandall calls "the great American cross-country ski-sport hero"—turned the race over to a nonprofit foundation, which now is supported by dozens of sponsors and entry fees and maintains a year-round storefront on Main Street.

Hayward's downtown is no little Aspen, though there is a mural of snow-capped mountains on the chalet-style facade of Duffy Law Offices, and cappuccino is served at the Big Mill and Backroads Coffee and Tea.

More typical is West's Dairy, in a marvelously old-fashioned building of candy-red bricks and, two blocks away, the Moccasin Bar, otherwise known as taxidermy heaven. Cal Johnson's muskie is mounted there—it's about the size of a skinny sixth-grader—and dozens of stuffed bear cubs, beavers and chipmunks who appear to play poker, drink beer and sing barbershop ditties in glass cases along the walls.

More big stuffed things glare over the tables at Coop's Pizza, three blocks up the street. From there, it's three blocks and a walk around Shue's Pond Park to the Lumberman's Mansion Inn, a Queen Anne showplace built for the local sawmill manager in 1887, when Hayward was a logging town.

Hayward is a lumber town even today; visitors heading into it are likely to be sandwiched between flatbed trucks piled high with logs, headed for the Louisiana Pacific waferboard plant. In the summer, Scheers Lumberjack Shows on the shore of Lake Hayward, just south of downtown, combine the old arts of tree-climbing and log-rolling with clowning and showmanship.

From the Lumberman's Mansion, it's just a block to Main Street, which doubles as the finish line of the Birkie.

To Wendy Sanders, who runs the inn with her sister, Jan Blaedel, Hayward is neither a ski town nor a muskie town.

"The most precious thing up here is the lakes and forest; you just can't beat it, summer or winter," she says. "When I'm out skiing on a frozen lake, and I can hear the ice rumbling, I feel so overwhelmed by the magnificence of nature. That's what makes Hayward famous."

❂ TRIP TIPS: Hayward

- **Events:** Winterfest, first weekend of February.
  American Birkebeiner, last full weekend in February.
  Musky Festival, third weekend in June.
  Honor the Earth Powwow, second or third weekend in July.
  Lumberjack World Championships, last full weekend in July.
  Chequamegon Fat Tire Festival, second weekend in September.

- **Trails:** Birkebeiner and Hatchery—From the junction of highways 63 and 77, drive east on 77 for two miles, and turn left on Hatchery Road. The Birkie trailhead starts just south of the parking lot. The scenic Hatchery trail, which has .4 km, 1.15 km and 1.9 km loops, is lighted until 10 P.M. daily for night skiing. No fees; donations accepted. A $1 booklet on other ski trails within an hour of Hayward is sold at New Moon Shop, just north of the intersection of highways 77 and 63.

- **Telemark:** The downhill ski resort, (800) 472-3001, 20 miles north near Cable, has 65 kilometers of cross-country trails. The fee is $8.

- **Attractions:** The National Fresh Water Fishing Hall of Fame, home of a 45-foot-high fiberglass muskie and other giant fish, is open April 15 through Nov. 1. Admission is $4–$1.50.

- **Accommodations:** Lumberman's Mansion Inn, (715) 634-3012. Five rooms furnished with antiques, $75–$95. Mustard Seed B&B, (715) 634-2908. Five rooms and a cottage, $60–$95. There are dozens of summer resorts in the area. For the Birkie, rooms in a 100-mile radius are booked solid. The Birkebeiner Foundation keeps a list of available lodgings and sometimes knows of cancellations. (800) 872-2753, (800) 722-3386 (in Wisconsin), (715) 634-5025.

- **Information:** Hayward Chamber of Commerce, (800) 724-2992 or (715) 634-8662.

New Glarus

A town with one foot in the Alps

In 1845, a city father addressed 193 nervous people in the Swiss canton of Glarus: "Diligence and eagerness for work, these two glorious national virtues of the Glarnese—take them with you, dear departing fellow citizens, into your new fatherland," boomed Caspar Jenny.

And with that, the crowded canton shooed out the new emigrants, some so impoverished their mountain villages had to pay traveling expenses. But they had a place to land: 1,200 acres in the rolling hills of south-central Wisconsin, chosen by two trustees of the Glarus Emigration Society, who then had to quickly build 14 one-room cabins to house the 108 people who arrived on their heels.

The colonists suffered and starved at first; they were weavers and didn't know a thing about farming. But, being Swiss, they worked hard and saved their pennies. Today, New Glarus is a flourishing middle-American farm town with one foot in the Alps: In 1995, 4,500 visitors from Switzerland poured in to help the town celebrate its 150th anniversary.

"What's interesting is they continue to be very interested in us," says Lila Dibble, a descendant of the emigrants and a guide at the Swiss Historical Village. "They feel very responsible for us."

Wisconsin 69 crosses the Little Sugar River and rolls into town, flat and without fanfare. No mountains, but look— there's a sprawling Swiss chalet, a hotel with wooden balconies and window boxes with cascading geraniums. And another chalet that's a bank. And one for the chiropractor, too.

Up a gentle incline a block away, in the downtown, there are Swiss flags and more half-timbered beams. Old Germanic platitudes unfurl in Gothic script across plaster facades: "Um froehlich zu sein braucht es wenig, und doch wer froehlich ist, der ist ein Koenig": "One needs little to be happy, and he who is happy, is a king."

I walk into the Glarner Stube, whose heavy wood beams and coziness give it the feel of a Bavarian pub, except the people next to me at the bar are drinking martinis and watching NFL football. A spry bartender who looks just like Kaiser Wilhelm fetches me an Edel-Pils made just down the road by the New Glarus Brewing Co.; it's marvelous, fruity and smooth.

Under a mounted crossbow—this is William Tell territory— I eat pastetles, slices of veal, pork and chicken in a pastry shell with fresh mushrooms in a wine cream sauce; and roesti, the Swiss national dish of potatoes made with aged cheese—"very aged," notes my waitress, Betty, with an arched eyebrow.

The next morning, I install myself in the pleasant tearoom above the New Glarus Bakery, looking forward to a classic European breakfast of crusty hard rolls, butter, jam and strong coffee, which is so very good I ask if there's a trick to making it; but, if there is, the waitress won't reveal it.

Across the street, people have arrived for Sunday brunch at the 1853 New Glarus Hotel, filling the glassed-in wooden balconies. The warm weather has slowed business at the picturesque Choco-Laden, which sells chocolate and other meltable delicacies, but Mrs. Lackovich's Christmas House is filled with women, oohing and aahing over the large collection of Central European blown-glass ornaments, made from 19th century molds.

From a half-timbered depot, bicyclists are heading south on the scenic Sugar River State Trail, which follows the river 23 miles to Brodhead. I drive a few blocks to the Swiss Historical Village, where Lila Dibble shows me and a half-dozen other tourists the exhibits of cheese and textiles contributed by contemporary Glarnese. She makes a point about homesickness by showing us two waist-high relief maps, one of the lovely but gentle hills around New Glarus, and one of the severe peaks around Glarus, a canton southeast of Zurich.

"The colonists were happy to be here, but they missed the mountains," she says. "Here, there was a feeling the whole world could look in on them."

She leads us to a tiny pioneer cabin, a beekeeping house, a school and a cheese factory, with an enormous copper vat brought by oxen from Milwaukee in the late 1860s and still used to make cheese during festivals. As a child, Dibble says, she played around the pot, abandoned in a decaying building; and like most children before World War II, she could not speak English when she entered kindergarten.

"Now, the town is less than 50 percent Swiss, but before the war, it must've been 80 percent," she says. "Young people were better educated after the war and saw better opportunities elsewhere."

The building of quaint Alpine facades began only in the 1930s and accelerated after the war, she says, as the town tried to hang onto its heritage.

Today, New Glarus attracts crowds, especially for its Heidi Festival in June and Wilhelm Tell Festival over Labor Day. Everyone likes it: Downtown, I pass a cadre of tough-looking sightseers on Harleys, and I stop to chat with a 75-year-old man who has driven up from Chicago in an antique Bentley he bought from his Swiss cousin. Weekend bicyclists and shoppers cruise First Street.

The colonists had nothing. But their town, a century and a half later, has it all.

✪ TRIP TIPS: New Glarus

- **Accommodations:** New Glarus has many festivals that fill the town, so reserve ahead. Chalet Landhaus has comfortable rooms with Swiss accents, $64–$145, $49–$115 in winter. (800) 944-1716. The New Glarus Hotel downtown is historic, but the six rooms are smaller and noisier, $37.50–$59.50. (800) 727-9477. Among the many B&Bs is the Shaker-style Linden Inn, $60–$80, (608) 527-2675.
- **Events:** Little Switzerland Winter Festival, second weekend in February.
  Community Fest, Memorial Day weekend.
  Swiss Polkafest, first full weekend in June.
  Heidi Festival, last full weekend of June.
  Volksfest, first Sunday in August.
  Wilhelm Tell Festival, Labor Day weekend.
  Octoberfest, Columbus Day weekend.
  Antique Show, third weekend in October.
- **Tours:** New Glarus Brewing Co., across Highway 69 from Village Park at County Road W, gives free tours between noon and 4:30 P.M. Saturdays year-round that includes samples of its Edel-

Pils lager, Uff-da Bock and nine seasonal beers; (608) 527-5850. Upright Swiss Embroideries, 1100 Second St., allows visitors to watch lace production on huge imported looms Monday through Friday; (608) 527-2515.
- **Sugar River State Trail:** Bikes can be rented at the headquarters in New Glarus, which also supplies a shuttle service. Cross-country skiing in winter. Daily trail pass is $3, seasonal $10. (608) 527-2334. From downtown, a paved bike path leads to New Glarus Woods State Park.
- **Museums:** Swiss Historical Village, daily May–October, admission $5, $1 for those 6–13.
  Chalet of the Golden Fleece, open daily May–October, $3, $1 for those 6–17.
- **Information:** (800) 527-6838.

Wisconsin Caves
Repositories of stalactites and legend

Ebenezer Brigham had a golden touch, but he never knew it. His first lucky strike was lead. In the late 1820s, Brigham traveled from Massachusetts to Galena, Ill., which already was crowded with other miners. So he walked northeast, stuck his shovel in the ground and found lead near the Blue Mounds, two conical, bluish-gray hills that were landmarks for Indians and pioneers.

He bought the land in 1828 and became the first settler of Dane County, which now includes Madison, and he and the town of Blue Mounds prospered—in mid-century, geography books described Milwaukee as "a village on Lake Michigan, east of Blue Mounds."

The land was still in the family in 1939, when Charles Brigham leased a quarry to the government. The workmen were in a hurry and used 1,600 pounds of black powder to blast the face off the quarry wall. Five thousand tons of limestone blew into the air, but when the dust settled, much of it was gone.

Instead, they saw two holes—entrances to an astonishing cavern.

Brigham leased the cave to a banker and a music teacher in nearby Mount Horeb, who opened it the next year to crowds, many of whom came on special excursion trains from Chicago. Today, Cave of the Mounds, the region's only cave that stays open all year, is owned by Ebenezer Brigham's great-great-grandniece and still is drawing crowds.

I visited on a balmy afternoon in August, walking down into a lush bowl and over a little stone bridge to the visitors center. All was quiet but for the sawing of cicadas, the tiny plops of falling acorns and the gurgle of a creek, its banks planted with perennials.

In a receiving room, a short video told the story: one or two million years ago, rain, gases and acid began to eat cavities in a thick layer of limestone, once the silty muck on the bottom of an inland sea. Underground streams carved corkscrew tunnels, picking up minerals that colored the walls—manganese for purple and black, iron oxide for shades of red, calcite for white—and the stalactites that formed over eons of dripping.

A young guide named John took our group into the caverns, admonishing us not to touch, though the smoothly gelatinous surfaces, like the back of a wet hippo, made it almost irresistible. We walked by stalagmites ("g" as in ground; for stalactites, "c" as in ceiling) that looked like the stubby trolls found in Mount Horeb, and Onyx Ridge, a 17-foot-tall stalagmite on which ancient rivulets had created the veiled-lady effect used by marble sculptors.

We finally got to touch a knob of calcite, burnished gold by thousands of fingers, and headed down a winding passageway to an area where John pointed out "bacon-strip" stalactites and wavy sheets of flowstone.

"It looks smooth, but it's as slippery as wet sandpaper," he said. We passed "bleeding" stalactites clinging to the wall; diamond stalactites, the light refracting through drops of water clinging to their tips; and soda-straw stalactites, hollow, half-inch growths born after the big blast.

With a flick of the light, John showed us the phosphorescence of pure calcite, then led us to to a massive column that looked a tyrannosaurus shinbone. For a finale, we gaped at several diorama-like rooms off the passageway, glowing with glorious clusters of formations.

A couple of days later, I drove west along the Wisconsin River to another cave, the picturesquely named Kickapoo Indian Caverns.

The first whites to see it, said my guide, Kathy, were soldiers from Fort Crawford in nearby Prairie du Chien, and others looking for lead in the mid-1800s. For years before that, the caverns had been used by local Kickapoo as a shelter in winter, when 50 degrees felt warm. She pointed out walls stained by smoke, blown by drafts right out the opening, now covered by the shop.

I could touch whatever I wanted, and lead-pencil inscriptions—"Edna and Fred, 1897"—showed I wasn't the first: What covered bridges were to the lovers of Madison County, these caverns were to those of Wauzeka.

"You can see who was going together; it's kind of fun," Kathy said. "They'd come out and show their grandkids."

We walked under a white cross strung from the ceiling— "We don't know who put it there, but we've had five weddings"—and past the seafoam-colored Chamber of Lost Water, a pure, spring-fed pool from which the Kickapoo drank. She pointed out a mastodon bone imbedded in the ceiling, and a "spoon" on the wall that, at first, I didn't believe wasn't real.

The Kickapoo link is no gimmick, says cave owner Delores Gaidowski; once, thousands lived near the caverns, from the 1500s until they were sent to Texas by the U.S. government. They ended up in Kansas, Oklahoma and Mexico, she says, and occasionally their descendants visit.

"Nothing's been written about them," Gaidowski says with regret. "They were very quiet, farmers and small-game hunters. They came from the east and Michigan and were pushed down here. Then they were sent away, and that was that."

✪ TRIP TIPS: Wisconsin Cave Tours

The temperature of caves is about 50 degrees year-round. Bring a warm jacket and wear comfortable shoes.

- **Cave of the Mounds:** Twenty miles west of Madison, next door to Little Norway. Open daily from March 15 to Nov. 15 and weekends year-round. Admission $8; $4 children 5–12. (608) 437-3038.

- **Kickapoo Indian Caverns:** 20 miles east of Prairie du Chien, near Wauzeka. Open daily mid-May through October. Admission $7; $3.50 children 5–12. (608) 875-7723.

  Another cave is in west-central Wisconsin, 13 miles southeast of I-94's Ellsworth exit, near Spring Valley. Crystal Cave is open daily Memorial Day to Labor Day, weekends in April–May and September–October. Admission is $6, $4 children 5–12. Candlelight tours from the weekend before Thanksgiving to Christmas Eve, $3. Large population of bats. (800) 236-CAVE, (715) 778-4414.

Little Norway
A flowering of culture

Vergeane the tour guide stands erect and proud in her embroidered bunad, ushering her group of tourists, mostly Japanese, around the scattering of buildings on the floor of an idyllic valley.

Flowers grow everywhere; a stream gurgles nearby. This beautiful but largely untillable valley, so much like Norway, once was the home of Telemark emigrant Osten Haugen. Between 1856 and 1920, it provided a hardscrabble existence for him, his wife and four daughters, who lived in a two-room cabin whose tiny size amazes modern visitors.

Haugen's farmstead today is Little Norway, an open-air museum. Chicago businessman Isak Dahle bought it in 1926, restored the buildings and furnished them from his collection of Norwegian antiques. In 1935, he installed its stunning Stavkirke, a reproduction of a medieval church that was built in Norway for the 1893 Chicago World's Fair, and in 1937 he opened it to the public.

Little Norway is in a lovely part of southwest Wisconsin that includes Cave of the Mounds, Blue Mound State Park and the 39-mile Military Ridge State Trail. Today, it is tourist country. People come to take a Troll Stroll in nearby Mount Horeb, to shop for antiques and to see the Stavkirke, with its dragon's heads like those on the prows of Viking ships.

But not that long ago, this was the promised land for a people who asked for nothing more than 40 acres and a future. Their descendants, though prosperous now, haven't forgotten the homeland and its traditions.

In 1814, Norway was packed to the gills. Most of its people were crowded onto the 3 percent of land that then could be cultivated. Many young people, even small landholders, had a bleak future. Norway was beautiful, and the love of its fiords and green valleys lived deep in the souls of its people. But the Norwegians had to leave.

By 1915, Norway had lost 750,000 people to the United States, contributing, after Ireland, the highest percentage of its population to the new country. One of the first places to which the immigrants flowed was southwest Wisconsin. They settled in its valleys, farmed, and learned English. But the church, a Norwegian-language press and cultural societies kept the old traditions alive.

Today, this heritage is thriving. Near Coon Valley is Norskedalen, a 400-acre open-air museum and arboretum run by a nonprofit foundation. There's a modern nature and heritage center for workshops and cultural programs, and across a creek, a pioneer homestead of buildings moved from nearby farms. Old-country traditions are kept alive: Lefse and flatbread are made on an old wood stove, wool is woven on a loom and the garden is tilled by horses.

And every year in May comes an explosion of Norwegian culture—parades of regional costumes, rosemaling, folk dancing, lefse-baking—to celebrate Syttende Mai, the May 17 Constitution Day.

Tens of thousands will come to Stoughton, said to hold the largest celebration outside Norway, and to other towns settled by Norwegian immigrants. What they will celebrate is not the mere signing of a document but the end of a time during which Norway's national identity, language and culture were suppressed, a time 19th century playwright Henrik Ibsen called Norway's "400 years' night."

Between 1380 and 1814, Norway was Denmark's doormat, a hinterland seen mainly as a source of taxes, timber and young men to fight Denmark's wars. But in 1814, amid the debris of Denmark's losing position in the Napoleonic Wars,

Norway pulled off a velvet revolution, declaring independence and adopting the most democratic constitution in Europe.

It wasn't really independent until 1905, when it dissolved its ties to Sweden, and the ascendance of King Harald V to the throne in 1991 marked the first time since 1387 Norway's king was born in Norway. But that May 17 marked the beginning of a new national pride.

That's why today, in the tiny town of Stoughton, famous for its Norwegian Dancers, teen-age boys who twirl around in breeches have more prestige than football stars. Why skilled woodcarvers have turned Mount Horeb into the Troll Capital. Why a Chicago businessman would buy a deserted farm in a picturesque valley and name it Nissedahle, valley of the elves.

And why, last but not least, you can buy lye-soaked cod along with hot dogs and cotton candy at a Syttende Mai festival. Among Norwegians, traditions die hard.

✪ TRIP TIPS: Syttende Mai and Heritage Sites

- **Syttende Mai:** It's pronounced SEH-tend-ah MY. All of the towns below celebrate on the closest weekend to May 17.

  Stoughton, Wis., southeast of Madison. Call (608) 873-7912 for a listing of the many events.

  Spring Grove, Minnesota's first Norwegian settlement. (507) 498-5221.

  Woodville, Wis., just off I-94 near Baldwin, (715) 698-2355.

  Westby, Wis., near Norskedalen, (608) 634-4193, (608) 637-2575.

- **Little Norway:** It's just west of Mount Horeb, off Highway 18-151. Admission is $6 adults, $2 children 6–12. It's open daily mid-April to October. (608) 437-8211. For a copy of a visitor's guide to the area, call (800) 279-9472.

- **Norskedalen:** It's two miles north of Coon Valley, Wis. Admission is $3 adults, $2 children 6–12. Guided tours are given daily April 15 through October; the center is open Monday through Friday year-round.

  Five miles of skiing and hiking trails lead into corridors of tall red pines, through restored prairie meadows and up hillsides. They're open dawn to dusk year-round.

  Events include Midsummer, usually the third weekend in June; Threshing Bee, last Saturday of September; and Old-Fashioned Christmas, first weekend in December. (608) 452-3424.

Kickapoo Valley
A crooked river amid splendid isolation

They call it the crookedest river in the world.

On a topographic map, the Kickapoo is a tight little squiggle, the Lombard Street of southwest Wisconsin. Its inability to flow straight for more than a few yards is nearly equal to a 2-year-old's ability to sit still for more than a few minutes.

Maybe that's why, along with its shallowness and gentle current, the Kickapoo is known as one of the best family canoeing rivers in Wisconsin. Each turn brings a new vista; it's nearly impossible to lose interest.

Even for a toddler.

On one weekday in late June, we started out from Ontario, not far from the Elroy-Sparta State Trail, with a 2-year-old who had never been on water. Swaddled up to his ears in life-jacket, tethered to his father by nylon rope, he sat motionless, a little orange Michelin man. Ninety percent of the river is only waist-deep, but the river was flowing faster than usual due to recent rains, and we weren't taking any chances.

Three canoes full of local high-school kids bumbled out of the landing ahead of us, making a doubly crooked path in the crooked river and giggling at their mistakes. Then the river's bends swallowed them, leaving us to glide in silence past grassy banks and mud walls riddled with bird holes.

Soon, the terrain changed. Sandstone outcroppings, twisted cedars barely hanging onto their tops, began to cast their cold shadows over the narrow river. We paddled this way and that, a C-stroke here, a J-stroke there; "Kickapoo" is Algonquin for "the one who goes there, then here."

We looked for blue heron, deer, beaver, even a raccoon—supposedly, wildlife is abundant—but our predecessors had frightened off everything but the butterflies. But, as we rounded one bend, we did see what looked like a giant otter splashing around on his back. It was Dennis Davison, who often canoes the Kickapoo. For several miles, he paddled nearby, offering tips on negotiating fallen trees and sandbars. One tree was so large we were surprised we didn't find the teen-agers impaled on its branches; we didn't have such an easy time getting around it ourselves.

Then we spotted an observation post high on the ridge in front of us, in nearby Wildcat Mountain State Park. Soon, we were at the lower park landing, a three-hour trip we did in two hours and 15 minutes, and the van from Kickapoo Paddle Inn was pulling up to fetch us, right on time.

The teen-agers were there, too, and one boat was full of muddy water. "We tipped!" wailed a girl. Moral: The Kickapoo isn't tough to canoe, but you should know how to steer.

We had paddled six miles. The winding van ride back to Ontario covered 3½ miles; as the crow flies, it's barely two. During our trip, we had paddled in all four directions of the compass.

The Kickapoo surges out of a vast watershed 11 miles north of Ontario and, by the time it joins the Wisconsin River at Wauzeka, 70 highway miles later, it has meandered 120 miles.

The Kickapoo is not only the crookedest river, says Bob Sullivan, who owns Mr. Duck rentals in Ontario, it's the second-oldest—or so he's been told by faculty and students at the University of Wisconsin-La Crosse, who occasionally come to examine it.

"This valley has been unglaciated during the last two ice ages," Sullivan says. "If you look at old maps of the glaciers, you see that they surround our valley, for some reason, but don't go into it. If the Ice Age created the Mississippi, and if this was unglaciated, who's to say it's not that old?"

Because the drifting glaciers never flattened this area, the terrain around the Kickapoo is a nearly mountainous series of high ridges and deep valleys. "Who would have thought there'd be views like this here?" my husband said, as we drove along small country roads.

One of the best is 8.6-mile Rustic Road 56, which follows the spine of a high ridge between Ontario and Rockton, laying out panoramas of far-off valleys and passing an 1855 chinked log cabin and Amish farms.

Vernon County has the largest Amish settlement in Wisconsin; they began arriving in the late 1960s from Ohio. From our cottage near La Farge, we often walked along a ridge lined with their farms, from which the men usually waved at us from their horse-drawn threshers and wagons.

At the entrances to many of the farms, notices announce

goods or crafts for sale, though never on Sunday. Visitors are welcome to stop by for eggs, maple syrup or, if they're lucky, a bit of conversation.

✪ TRIP TIPS: Kickapoo Valley

- **Getting there:** The Upper Kickapoo Valley is 25 miles south of Sparta and the intersection of interstates 90 and 94.
- **Canoe rentals:** Mr. Duck, Ontario, (608) 337-4711; Drifty's Fas-trip, Ontario, (608) 337-4288. Costs start at $14 for short trips, including all equipment and shuttle service, to $28–$45 for the two-day, 24-mile trip to La Farge. Camping is allowed on the shore, most of which is federally owned. For summer weekends, canoes should be reserved in advance. There can be canoe jams on Saturdays; weekday canoeists are more likely to see wildlife.
- **Accommodations:** The Inn at Wildcat Mountain, a B&B in a 1910 Greek Revival home, is within walking distance of the canoe landing in Ontario. Four rooms that share 1½ baths, $45–$75. (608) 337-4352.

  Trillium, an isolated B&B on a farm above La Farge, is a short walk from a series of Amish farms on a scenic ridge. A rustic one-bedroom cottage and a three-bedroom house, $55–$70. (608) 625-4492.

  Viroqua Heritage Inn, an 1890 Victorian in Viroqua, a larger town in a flatter part of the county. Four rooms, $50–$175. (608) 637-3306.

  Thirty campsites are available at Wildcat Mountain State Park, (608) 337-4775.
- **Bicycle trails:** The Elroy-Sparta and 400 state trails are nearby, and the county roads are ideal for bicycling, though don't expect a flat ride. Vernon County, (608) 637-2575, sends out brochures on inn-to-inn bicycling and bike routes.
- **Information:** Hidden Valleys Association, (608) 725-5867; Kickapoo Valley Association, (608) 625-2020. *Best Canoe Trails in Southern Wisconsin* (Wisconsin Trails, $10.95) contains more details about the Kickapoo and many other rivers.

Spring Green
Spectacles for brows high and low

There's only one town in the Midwest that can call itself a
nirvana, a mecca, a regular Wall Drug for aesthetes and
philistines alike.

Meet Spring Green, Wisconsin, equal-opportunity tourist
attraction. The town of Spring Green is a small, unassuming
settlement just north of the broad Wisconsin River. It's dis-
tinguished mainly by The Post, which claims to be the oldest
continuously operating restaurant in Wisconsin, and some interesting art galleries.

On the other side of the river, however, are monuments to
egos as nakedly unshakable as the limestone outcroppings
around which they're built. Meet Frank Lloyd Wright, genius
but no gentleman. The architect was born in the valley in 1867
and reappeared in 1911 with the wife of a client, having abandoned his own wife and six children in Oak Park, Ill.

Taliesin, the vast hillside home he built for his mistress, is
considered by some to be the greatest single building in
America. Its opening for tours in 1992 was accompanied by a
plea for $24 million—the cost of shoring up stone and wood ar-
ranged by a man too haughty to touch a level.

Now meet Alex Jordan, visionary and creep. He was a convicted blackmailer who abandoned his family, says the recent,
unauthorized biography *House of Alex,* which also reports that
the house Jordan became famous for initially was an effort by
his father to spite their architect neighbor.

The House on the Rock, too, is a masterpiece—of a magnificent cheesiness—created by a man whose personal vision
was a pubescent Twilight Zone of bordellos and teeming
bazaars. Cheesy—but for every Wright acolyte, there are many
more dying to see this.

The Frank Lloyd Wright Visitors Center has a spire straight
out of "The Jetsons" and is tinted with the colors Wright loved,
barn red and the rich ocher of limestone. Inside, reverent visitors are gazing at the long bank of windows facing the river,
the cross-hatched beams, the rough stone fireplace.

I've never been fond of Wright—perhaps all those ugly '60s knockoffs soured me—but even I can feel a serenity born of light and space. Wright designed the building as a restaurant, and one corner still is a cafe.

I could join the $7 tour of the Hillside Studio—"best introduction to Wright and his work"—but instead, I drive farther up the road to the American Players Theatre and buy a ticket to that evening's performance of the 1773 comedy *She Stoops to Conquer.* The troup's other three plays are Shakespeare, but this one is by Oliver Goldsmith, and it's wickedly funny. With a packed house, I see it under the stars in the repertory troupe's amphitheater in the woods.

And as it turns out, I get a little tour the next morning around breakfast at the Hill Street B&B, where several guests have inside knowledge of Wright and his buildings. An older woman from Illinois turns out to be the daughter of a student at the 1902 Hillside School, a finishing school run by Wright's aunts on the Taliesin grounds. The school was put out of business, Pat says, when the girls' mothers objected to the love nest next door—though things got much more lurid later, when Wright's mistress, her two children and four employees were hacked to death by a deranged servant.

"On the tour, I asked the guide, 'You know the real story, don't you?'" Pat says. "She said, 'Yes, but we can't tell that.'"

Barbara, Pat's companion, warns me about my plan to visit the House on the Rock—"You see it, and you see it, and you see it," she said. "I've never been so tired in all my life."

But the House on the Rock is like a train wreck—you can't not look. I walk quickly through the real house, built in the '40s. The rest Jordan added on over the years in a maze of dark rooms, filled with the tinny racket of music machines. At one point, the music fades and I am alone, surrounded by old dentistry tools, antique cash registers, ships in bottles—and a jester with uncannily lifelike eyes. I wonder if a horror movie had ever been set at House on the Rock.

The last half of the tour is the "Eclectic Era," when, it seems, Jordan began scouring the world for high kitsch. It's eye-popping. In the three-story carousel room, department-store mannequins with wings and breast-baring togas dangle over 20,000 bulbs glowing red and white, 269 rotating animals and George the attendant, who gamely bears the deafening music.

"Oh boy, I wish that thing had a volume button," he says, grateful for a little conversation.

I escape into the relative serenity of a fine collection of dollhouses—Queen Anne, Tudor, log-cabin, you name it—then cases of miniature circuses and a wonderfully quirky series of machines made for the windows of jewelry stores in the late 1930s and early 1940s—scuba divers, swamis, even the Sphinx, all pushing diamonds at the push of a button.

I finally emerge, dazed, and before I have time to mull things over, a video in the gift shop does it for me. "A lot of people say Alex Jordan was insane—'Where did he get his ideas?'" the narrator intones. "That's a good question—and we'll never know the answer."

✪ TRIP TIPS: Spring Green

- **House on the Rock:** Open mid-March to the last full weekend in October and for a scaled-down holiday tour from mid-November to early January. Admission is $13.50 adults, $8.50 ages 7–12, $3.50 ages 4–6. Holiday tickets: $8, $4, $1. (608) 935-3639.

- **American Players Theatre:** Season is mid-June through September, Tuesday–Sunday. Tickets are $16.50–$29. Gourmet picnics and wine tastings are among special events. (608) 588-2361.

- **Frank Lloyd Wright tours:** Tours of sites from May through October, $7–$50. Reserve Taliesin tours in advance. The visitors center stays open until just before Christmas. (608) 588-7900.

- **Lodgings:** Hill Street B&B, seven attractive rooms, $65–$75, (608) 588-7751.

  Silver Star, nine miles out of town in country, handsome new inn with 10 rooms and cafe, $95–$135. (608) 935-7297.

  The Springs Golf Club Resort, a modern Wrightian golf club resort, with luxury suites across from theater, near Frank Lloyd Wright visitors center. $145–$165 April 1 to early June; then $165–$185 through September, and $120–$135 through March. A 15 percent service charge is added to room rates. (800) 822-7774.

- **Information:** (800) 588-2042.

Mineral Point
An intriguing pocket of Cornwall

In the early 1830s, the desperately poor miners of Cornwall, on England's rocky western tip, heard about lead deposits in America's Michigan Territory, at a place called Mineral Point.

Indians were first to scoop the shiny nuggets out of the earth. They were followed in 1827 by eager frontiersmen, who often lived in the "badger holes" they dug in their search for "mineral"—in what later became Wisconsin, the badger state.

But the Cornish were skilled miners, and they were able to sink much deeper pits. Many of the first arrivals staked claims and did well, though, in 1848, the gold rush siphoned off much of their ranks and the price of lead dropped.

The Cornish might have been absorbed into the local melting pot and forgotten, except for one thing: Because of an old-country tradition that granted a three-generation lease of land to those who could put up a house in 24 hours—meaning everyone had to help—the Cornish were expert stonemasons. They took the limestone and dolomite of the surrounding ridges and valleys and fashioned cottages that resembled those of their homeland. They also brought Celtic superstitions and had a penchant for names that sound whimsical to the American ear.

Today, both cottages and idioms are preserved at Pendarvis on Shake Rag Street, where visitors sometimes may find pasties and figgyhobbin cooking and storytellers in the kiddleywink telling of piskies and knackers.

Pendarvis, named after an estate in Cornwall, is a Wisconsin historic site, and in summer, costumed guides give daily tours of the restored cottages. I was lucky; the day I visited, Mark Knipping, Pendarvis director at the time, was giving his annual walking tour of Merry Christmas Mine hill, where Cornish miners once dug for lead ore. There was always a miner working at the top of the hill, so when the women in the cottages below had dinner ready, they would catch his attention by waving a dish towel, and he would pass the word.

Knipping was a mother lode of information, providing narration as we climbed past a shallow trench dug in the 1820s ("the frontiersmen who dug them were called suckers, because they came when the fish ran"); a pippin apple tree ("It's not native to the area; the seed rode up in a miner's lunch-bucket"); a circa-1850 Cornish counting house ("It's like the nursery rhyme, 'Four-and-twenty blackbirds, baked in a pie'") and a rusty, 1,500-pound ore can, which miners were paid 8 cents to fill at least 40 times a day ("It was a hard way to make a living, but it paid better than anything else").

Zinc was mined until the late 1970s; there's still plenty of ore, but processing can't meet environmental standards.

After Knipping took the other members of the group off to look at a badger hole, I went back to Pendarvis for the regular tour. Elizabeth, my guide, wore a flimsy white bonnet and a blue apron, and talked about the people who once lived in the low-ceilinged cottages. Because the government wanted the mineral lands at full-bore production—making lead shot, among other things—farming wasn't allowed. Therefore, villagers had to rely on heavily salted food brought from Galena, Illinois—pork, butter, treacle. Whatever they had was stuffed into a pasty—"If you couldn't see it, you could eat it"—which was a perfect miner's lunch; it was said you could drop it to the bottom of a mine shaft and it wouldn't break apart.

In many ways, the durable pasty was the savior of Cornish culture in southwest Wisconsin. The Cornish were long gone and the cottages run down when Robert Neal and Edgar Hellum rescued them from the well-meaning maws of the WPA in 1934, financing their restorations by selling pasties, saffron cake and clotted cream at a restaurant there until the state historical society took over in 1970.

Mineral Point has done well for itself, unlike many other mining villages in the area—Hardscrabble, Hoof Noggle, Nip and Tuck. The brick and stone facades of its sloping High Street seemed tailor-made for galleries and antiques stores, and that's what they hold.

I expected a crowd to be there on a sunny Saturday in September, but the streets were quiet. The entire downtown is an historic district. Passing storefronts advertising gourmet coffee and various bibelots, I arrived at the tidy Red Rooster Cafe, where proprietor Patti McKinley packed me a pasty (rhymes with "nasty") and cold beer to go. I took it to the city park where, in 1836, the Wisconsin territory was created and Henry Dodge became its first governor. The pasty—sirloin, potato, onion and rutabaga in a flaky crust—was filling but bland, which is why, nowadays, it's served with chili sauce.

Oh, and about those other Cornish names: Figgyhobbin is a sweet pastry with raisins and burnt-sugar sauce. A kiddley-wink is a pub; kiddle is liquor smuggled by pirates onto the rocky Cornwall coast, and a wink is what you had to give the bartender to get it. Piskies are good-natured elves; knackers are more like trolls, mythical creatures who lived underground and might play tricks on miners.

Mineral Point's Cornish have long been overshadowed by the Germans and Irish settlers who followed them. But with such colorful traditions, their culture was destined to live on.

❂ TRIP TIPS: Mineral Point

* **Events:** Real Antiques Show, second weekends in June and August.
  Art in the Park, second Saturday in August.
  Cornish Festival and Taste of Mineral Point, last weekend in September.
  Fall Art Tour, third weekend in October.
  Christmas Tour of Homes, Sunday after Thanksgiving.
* **Nightlife:** The Mineral Point Opera House shows movies on weekends and occasionally programs concerts. The Shake Rag Players present occasional plays.
* **Recreation:** The 47-mile Cheese Country Trail starts from the real mineral point, the convergence of two streams where lead remained on top of the soil. The trail is for hikers, ATVs and snowmobiles.
* **Accommodations:** The Cothren House, (608) 987-2612, has five rooms, $65–$125, on an estate that includes an 1853 stone house, 1840 guesthouse-summer kitchen and 1830s log cabin.
  Other B&Bs and motels: Duke House, (608) 987-2821; Knudson's Guest House, 987-2733; House of the Brau-Meister, (608) 987-2913; Wilson House, (608) 987-3600; Wm. A. Jones House, (608) 987-2337; Pick N Paw, (608) 987-3985; Point Motel, (608) 987-2733, and Redwood Motel, (608) 987-2117.
* **Pendarvis:** Open May through October. Tours are $5. There are many special events, including two Children's Days. (608) 987-2122.
* **Information:** Mineral Point Chamber of Commerce, (608) 987-3201.

9 A POCKET OF IOWA

Amana Colonies
From communalism to consumerism

There's a question often asked about Iowa's seven Amana Colonies: Are the Amana people Amish?

And no wonder—the people of the Amanas spoke German, lived simply and adhered faithfully to Scripture. But no, they never were Amish.

The people of the Amanas were German immigrants who came to Iowa in 1855. They were devoutly religious, as were many people of the time, but in addition they believed in Inspirationism—that God speaks to modern-day people through "Werkzeuge" (the German word for tools) rather than ordained ministers. The name they gave their Iowa settlement, "Amana," comes from the Bible and means "remain true."

The Amish—and in fact, the largest community of Amish west of the Mississippi lives only 30 miles south of the Amanas, around Kalona—take their name from Jacob Ammann, a bishop born many years before the Community of True Inspiration was founded in 1714. They were never communal, but the people of the Amanas were.

That is, until 1932.

That was the year of the Great Change. A disastrous fire, an exodus of young people and the Depression's crippling effect on trade led the villages to drop the communal system to which they had held for nearly a century.

Today, capitalism flourishes, especially in the town of Amana, lined with quaint brick storefronts. The areas in which the old workers once pooled their skills—weaving, woodcrafting, wine-making, cooking—have made a lasting name for the colonies, especially among tourists.

Now, where a kitchen boss once directed meals made for 10 families, restaurants serve family-style, setting out heaping platters of smoked pork chops, roast beef and bowls of corn, mashed potatoes and sauerkraut. On the November day

I visited, one of the best-known restaurants, the Ox Yoke Inn, was just recovering from an influx of 90 University of Iowa football players, treated to Thanksgiving dinner in Amana in the hopes they'd trounce the University of Minnesota that weekend (which they did, 45–3).

I often visit Amana, the busiest of the seven villages, on the day after Thanksgiving. At the Millstream Brewing Co., employees pour little mugs of lager, Schild Brau Amber and wheat beer, made according to old German purity laws, with no pasteurization and just four ingredients, hops, barley malt, yeast and water.

At the Amana Woolen Mill, huge Swiss looms whip through a blanket—Scottish tartans, pastel baby comforters, cotton thermals—every three minutes. Only blankets are made here; there are clothes for sale, but these, marked "Made for the Amana Woolen Mill" could be made anywhere.

At the Amana Furniture Shop, crowds of people study cherry armoires, walnut end tables, oak bed frames. All are made of solid wood, and there is no production line: As in the past, each artisan begins a project and sees it through to the end. The workshop is in the back, past the grandfather clocks in what once was the Amana Calico Works.

As might be expected in a colony of Germans, there also are wonderful Christmas stores. The best known is the Christmas Room, but I like Tiny Tim's Colony Christmas, which carries $4 blown-glass ornaments from Poland, wood-block puzzles from Czechoslovakia and tiny painted-wood ornaments from Germany.

Amana also is the home of the Museum of Amana History, and the next-door Noe House, one of the B&Bs that have sprung up like the dandelions the seven wineries use to make wine.

Bookkeeper Rosemarie Geiger shows me around the Noe House, first a communal kitchen, then a doctor's house, now four attractive bedrooms, a living room and a dining room. She smiles as she tells me that, today, most of the business owners come from outside the Amana Colonies, though not so much the employees.

Geiger, who was born in High Amana, has a noticeable German accent; her grown children, she says, have only slight accents. The values and traditions of the old colonies, she says, have changed. But she brightens when I ask about the craftsmanship for which the villages still are known.

"No, that stays," she says. "That hasn't changed. That can be handed down."

☉ TRIP TIPS: Amana Colonies

- **Events:** Maifest, first weekend of May.
    Bluegrass Music Festival, third weekend in July.
    Amana Festival of the Arts, second Saturday in August.
    Eisenfest, third weekend in September.
    Oktoberfest, first weekend in October.
    Founder's Day, second Saturday in November.
    Prelude to Christmas, first weekend in December.
- **Accommodations:** The Noe House Inn in Amana, four rooms, $55–$75. (319) 622-6350.
    The Guest House Motor Inn in Amana, (319) 622-3599, has 38 rooms, $43–$49, in two buildings, one modern and one an 1860 sandstone building once used as a communal kitchen. It offers winter packages that include a night's lodging plus dinner and lunch at the Ox Yoke Inn, $70–$80 per couple.
- **Theater:** The Old Creamery Theatre is a professional troupe that performs from May through December. (800) 352-6262.
- **Museum:** Walking tours leave daily from the museum, open mid-April to mid-November. (319) 622-3567.
- **Information:** (800) 245-5465, (319) 622-7622.

Kalona

Old World piety among the Amish

The Amish girl with the pale green eyes counted my money slowly, deliberately. I wondered why; obviously, I'd given her the exact change. Or maybe not.

"This is yours," the girl said softly, pushing a nickel toward me. Then she permitted herself a small smile.

At the rural Community Country Store near Kalona, Iowa, women in white muslin prayer caps and long dresses of navy and dark green share the narrow aisles with the worldly shoppers who drive in from nearby Iowa City.

Unlike other shops run by the Old Order Amish, this one welcomes the public. For those fascinated by the Amish lifestyle, which rejects vanity and materialism, a walk through this farmstead general store is a lesson in itself. Overhead are hooks on which kerosene lamps are hung at dusk; this branch of the Amish doesn't use electricity. On the shelves are open boxes of the utilitarian goods found in general stores a century ago—shoehorns, thimbles, socks—plus baked goods, toys and bins of flour.

What I noticed next were the prices, set to be within reach of the families who till the land nearby. I found a pair of sturdy, black-leather Hush Puppies for my son, $10.50; my husband found heavy Thinsulate gloves for $5.

Around Kalona, it's piety that's important, not profit. The Amish have farmed this land since 1846; with about 700 members and seven congregations, theirs is the largest Amish community west of the Mississippi.

As I drove away from the store, I passed horses and buggies clattering over the gravel; as I turned onto Highway 22 toward downtown Kalona, I saw a one-room Amish country school, one of eight in the area. A dozen small, black-clad figures tore around the back yard in a game of chase, while another group, in bonnets, stood watching.

In this pocket of southeast Iowa, the 19th century never faded into history. Or even the 16th century—the Amish, who believe in a literal interpretation of the Bible, are direct descendants of the Anabaptists, a Swiss group that believed Martin Luther and the other figures of the Protestant Reformation didn't go far enough in returning the church to Scripture.

And still today, women wear a covering on their heads (1 Cor. 11:5) and do not cut their hair (1 Cor. 11:6); men wear beards but not mustaches because, to their Germanic ancestors, mustaches suggested the military. The Amish, like their cousins the Mennonites, are staunch pacifists.

It's not so easy to spot a Mennonite in Kalona, though they compose perhaps half of the town of 2,000. They, too, descend from the Anabaptists, though their lifestyle is relatively modern; many are the children of Old Order Amish. There are sects even within the Amish. The New Order Amish use rub-

ber tires on their buggies; the Beachy Amish may drive cars—
black ones—and use telephones.

This rich Old World heritage has made a tourist attraction
out of downtown Kalona. People come to gape at the Amish
and their buggies and then duck into antique and gift shops—
or maybe it's the other way around. Two dozen shops sell
quilts, dried flowers, pottery, fudge, dolls and various collect-
ibles, though they all close on Sunday for the Sabbath.

Among collectors, Kalona is best-known for its quilts. In
April, the Kalona Quilt Show draws thousands of people from
all over the country. Marilyn Woodin of Woodin Wheel Antiques, which sponsors the show, hangs 320 new quilts by
local Amish and Mennonite women, $395–$850, and antique
quilts, $100–$5,000.

"We're very into helping people see these quilts as American women's art," she says. Her personal collection of 250
quilts from 1820 to 1940 is stored in the Kalona Quilt and Tex-
tile Museum, above her store.

The best way to get to know the Amish and Mennonite culture of Kalona is by taking the 5½-hour tour offered by the
Kalona Historical Society.

The first half-hour, over coffee and doughnuts, is devoted to
straightening out the difference between Amish and Mennonites, and someone will probably ask where the nearby Amana
Colonies figure in (they don't—though both originated as sep-
aratist German-speaking communities, the people of the
Amanas are offshoots of Lutherans and abandoned their communal lifestyle in 1932; the Amish cooperate, but are not
communal).

Then come demonstrations, such as rug-weaving or cheese-
making, and a meal in an Amish/Mennonite home, where organic meats, egg noodles, tapioca pudding and apple butter are
specialties. There's a visit to the Kalona Historical Village, an
open-air museum of buildings that includes an 1897 country
store, a schoolhouse, a post office and the 1879 railroad depot
around which the downtown grew.

The Iowa Mennonite Museum at the village is Kalona's
heirloom attic. Old tin toys, milk-glass dishes and 150-year-old
quilts are labeled with family names; Yoder and Miller are so
common the postmaster can't deliver mail without a middle
name. In another corner is an 1881 treadmill, on which dogs

or goats ran to pump water or separate milk. The treadmill, along with an outdoor bread oven and other antique equipment, is pressed into service once a year, at the Kalona Fall Festival, the town's biggest event.

If you want to know more about the Amish, Mary Brenneman of the chamber of commerce knows of an outgoing Amish couple who love to entertain.

"They're so open-minded, and they like to talk to people outside their own little world," she says. "They have people for meals and give them buggy rides. People just dearly enjoy it."

❂ TRIP TIPS: Kalona, Iowa

- **Getting there:** Kalona is 20 minutes south of Iowa City and Interstate 80.
- **Events:** Kalona Quilt Show, last Friday and Saturday of April.
  Kalona Days, second Saturday of July.
  Kalona Fall Festival, last Friday and Saturday of September.
  Christmas Tree walk, first Friday and Saturday of December.
- **Tours:** Heritage Tours are given Monday through Friday between April 15 and Oct. 15 by the Kalona Historical Society. Cost is $18. Call (319) 656-2519. At least 15 people are required, but individuals often can join groups; call ahead.
- **Museum:** Kalona Historical Village is open Monday through Saturday, 11 A.M. to 3 P.M. in winter and 10 A.M. to 4 P.M. in summer. Admission is $2.50 for adults, $1 for children 7–12.
- **Accommodations:** Heritage Haus B&B, (319) 656-3209. Two rooms with private baths in a renovated farmhouse, $50.
- **Information:** Kalona Area Chamber of Commerce, (319) 656-2660.

Iowa City
Old fossils in a university town

My hometown, Iowa City, is not a place that travel guides find easy to pin down. They mention Plum Grove, the restored home of Iowa's first territorial governor. They mention

Old Capitol, which served as the state's first capitol between 1842 and 1857.

Yawn. I toured these places on third-grade field trips, don't remember a thing, and don't care (though I'm very fond of Old Capitol's golden dome, whose far-off gleam often is the first thing visitors see).

There always have been many reasons to like this university town in southeast Iowa, but none of its attractions were particularly spectacular—until the summer of 1993, when a bolt from the heavens literally created one.

Remember the Big Flood? The rain clouds carried a silver lining for Iowa City: When floodwaters surged over the emergency spillway at Coralville Lake, outside the northeast end of town, they eroded 15 feet of bedrock deposits and exposed an ancient sea floor.

This rock floor, now known as the Devonian Fossil Gorge, provides a kind of photo-negative record of life 375 million years ago. It's unique because it's so easy to see: Littered on its surface are the imprints of the coral, sea lilies, worms and other primitive organisms that lived in a shallow, tropical sea.

In the first year after the gorge appeared, a million people came to see it, says Richard Rogers of the visitors center, who adds that the continuing stream of tramping feet on the soft limestone, formerly the mud on the ocean's bottom, doesn't bother park management.

"That rock is 1,000 feet deep," he says. "New fossils are appearing all the time. This rock is usually protected by soil; now that it's exposed, it's going to change continually."

On the chilly November day on which my family and I visited, dozens of people were roaming up and down the gorge, jumping from rock to rock, crouching to look closer. We found a fossil that looked exactly like a zipper—a crinoid, or sea lily, whose stems were strewn across the rock like knobby pick-up sticks. Elsewhere, we found shells that once enclosed the tentacles of brachiopods, chunks of coral, and lots of bizarre little bits we couldn't identify.

The rolling countryside around the fossil gorge, popular with serious bicyclists, includes nearby Lake Macbride State Park. I, too, used to ride my bike along these roads, and also 10 miles east to West Branch, home of a well-regarded museum and presidential library devoted to Depression-era President Herbert Hoover, who was born there.

Since then, Iowa has been converting abandoned rail lines to bicycle and hiking trails in a big way, and West Branch is a trailhead on what will be its longest, the 115-mile Hoover Nature Trail.

Leave a place for a few years, and look what happens. The University of Iowa's football team goes to Rose Bowls now, but the year I left was its first winning season in 19 years.

And yet, the enduring charm of this town is that the best things don't change: City Park, a long green spread along the Iowa River that includes a tiny, old-fashioned amusement park run by the same family since 1948. The student-run Bijou Theatre, a treasure that runs up to four films—art, foreign, vintage—every night. Bushnell's Turtle, a restaurant with polished oak booths, high ceilings and a veggie submarine sandwich better than any I can find elsewhere—and I've looked.

Iowa City's little old downtown was threatened by urban renewal for nearly two decades; it emerged almost unscathed but with a Holiday Inn and an enclosed mall on its periphery. These are easily ignored. When I visit, I head for the shops behind the old storefronts: Prairie Lights book store, which has added an espresso bar to the downtown's collection of coffeehouses. Masala, an East Indian restaurant and one of several that have erased Iowa City's old reputation as an awful restaurant town. Iowa Book and Supply, its small, recessed windows a reminder of the day its large ones were shattered in a Vietnam War riot.

Then I walk across Clinton Street toward Old Cap, one of five university buildings on the plaza known as the Pentacrest. Down the hill is the big Iowa Memorial Union, which houses the Bijou Theatre and the Iowa House, a university-run hotel that has rooms overlooking the Iowa River.

Along this gentle river, spanned by graceful old bridges, the buildings are lined up like diamonds on a choker: The University of Iowa Art Museum, its Max Beckmann triptych still leering at visitors along with newer, even more startling acquisitions. The boxy brick home of University Theaters. The imposing silver angles of Hancher Auditorium, a stop for the world's greatest performers and a virtual second home of the Joffrey Ballet, from which it has commissioned large works.

Iowa City is a pretty hip little town, but it doesn't toot its horn much. Since it was founded in 1937, the Iowa Writers Workshop always has brought in big-name teachers—Kurt Vonnegut, John Cheever, Robert Penn Warren—and turned out graduates who became big names—John Irving, Raymond Carver, Tracy Kidder, Jane Smiley.

The writers can be seen giving readings at Prairie Lights and other places around town. Along with the students in the UI Symphony, which gives free concerts at Hancher, and the many professional musicians and artists who have found Iowa City too comfortable to leave, they're among the many who enrich life in this town of 70,000.

Occasionally, when I lived there, one of the newly arrived Writers Workshop students from the East would express surprise there weren't pigs running in the streets and corn growing in front yards. We locals would simply chuckle indulgently.

We didn't care if Iowa City made barely a blip on the national radar. We had a swell place, and we knew it.

❂ TRIP TIPS: Iowa City

- **Accommodations:** Iowa House, $60–$89, (319) 335-3513, and Holiday Inn, $86–$150, (319) 337-4058. In an older district of brick streets, within walking distance of downtown, Hancher and City Park, are four B&Bs: Brown Street Inn, five rooms, $50–$85, (319) 338-0435; Golden Haug, four rooms, $68–$95; (319) 338-6452; Bella Vista, four rooms, $45–$75, (319) 338-4129; and Haverkamps' Linn Street Homestay, three rooms, $30–$45, (319) 337-4363.
- **Devonian Fossil Gorge:** Four miles north of town on Dubuque Street, turn right at the "Coralville Lake" sign and keep going. For more information, call (319) 338-3543.
- **Hancher Auditorium:** For a schedule of events, call (319) 335-1160. Hancher also handles the box office for University Theaters, which puts on a repertory festival each summer on the works of one playwright.
- **Bijou Theatre:** (319) 335-3257.
- **Information:** Iowa City and Coralville Visitors Bureau, (800) 283-6592.

10 Clowns, Trains and Voyageurs

Baraboo
The biggest circus museum on Earth!

During the last quarter of the last century, Wisconsin was earning its title as "mother of circuses."

In Baraboo, five sons of a German-born harness-maker named Ruengeling, ever since they'd seen their first circus act as children, had been putting on skits and routines for the locals. In 1884, they set off with their first tent, putting it up, selling tickets, then jumping into the ring to perform; in the show's biggest act, Al Ringling balanced a plow on his chin.

The circus grew, and by 1890, the Ringling brothers were competing with Barnum & Bailey. In 1907, Ringling bought its rival and became the biggest circus operation in the world.

Those were the days in Baraboo. Each winter, until 1918, the Ringling brothers returned to their quarters on the banks of the Baraboo River to repair wagons, train animals and rehearse new acts.

Today, this former Ringlingville is Circus World Museum, established in 1959, two years after the Ringling Bros. and Barnum & Bailey Circus abandoned its big top and moved to indoor arenas.

Here, in a 50-acre complex that lines both sides of the placid river, is preserved the spirit of the old circus, the wonder that made a crusty Ernest Hemingway call it "the only spectacle I know that, while you watch it, gives the quality of a truly happy dream."

There's a re-created Gargantua the Great, a gorilla with an evil sneer who was a house pet named Buddy before Ringling got hold of him and billed him as "the world's most terrifying creature." There's a fabulous collection of restored circus wagons, every inch of them covered with gilt eagles, mirrors, bare-breasted women and rearing horses. There's Clown Alley, including the well-used trunks and props of famous clowns—in the case of Felix Adler, who joined the Ringlings at age 12, a bird-cage hat and rhinestone rings the size of plums.

And, of course, there's the Big Top. In daily shows under a blue tent, Circus World Museum "takes you back in time to the golden age of the American circus." When we were there, the acrobatic Natasha undulated her way inside three hoops, sparkling in black sequins. In a "marvelous zoological fantasy," a white pony outfitted with a purple plume pranced amid clouds of smoke. Clowns with yellow derbies squashed onto red shocks of hair made bad puns and pratfalls.

It wasn't really the "golden age," in that the band relied on themes from recent Disney movies, and the dancers must have trained in a disco. But the high-wire walkers were classic. With flashing white smiles and skin-tight costumes, the Carrillos of Colombia walked over one another, balanced on a chair, played leapfrog and jumped rope to the relentless thump of a gong, all high on the wire, all without a net.

In the best act, a hobo trick rider picked a fight with a Fabio look-alike, skipping across the backs of three galloping ponies and using his hat as a guided missile. There was a juggler, pink ladies twirling on ropes, gymnasts from Guatemala, and what could be left?

The elephants, linchpin of any circus. P.T. Barnum made a fortune with an elephant who made his name, "Jumbo," a synonym for huge. Elephants have been a sensation ever since the first one arrived on U.S. shores in 1796, perhaps because, as one circus press agent noted, it's "the largest animal you'll ever see this side of delirium tremens."

Under the Circus World tent, three elephants walked tail in trunk, got up on stools and balanced on each other. One grabbed a dancer's leg in its trunk and twirled her around in a pirouette. Nothing spectacular, but irresistible.

On summer days, the Big Top shows are supplemented by a clown-makeup demonstration, street parade and magic show. Around the grounds are exhibits: The Cardiff giant, a faked "petrified man" that Barnum, when its owner wouldn't sell, faked again and put on display. A history of the sideshow, with photos of such early "freaks" as 685-pound Alice from Dallas, contortionist Shubert the Frog Boy and "half lady" Mlle. Gabriele, many of whom look like quite pleasant people. A miniature circus behind glass, where a pushed button makes an elephant wag its tail or a boy "sidewall"—slip under the tent to get in for free.

Many other stories are told at the big exhibit hall. "A Century of Spectacle" includes props of the early, cast-of-thousands theatrical pageants. And of course, there's the rags-to-riches stories of the Ringling brothers—eventually, all seven worked for the family circus—and a video about Gunther Gebel-Williams, the charismatic animal trainer who helped rejuvenate the circus after Irvin Feld bought it from John Ringling North in 1967.

Today, the circus is alive and well. It no longer shows painted ladies, or Lou Jacobs in a motorized bathtub, or blindingly gaudy parade wagons.

To see those things, go to Baraboo.

❂ TRIP TIPS: Baraboo

- **Circus World:** The live-show season runs from the first weekend of May through the weekend after Labor Day. Admission is $12 for adults, $6 for children 3–12. In July, the museum's restored wagons are loaded onto flatcars for the rail trip into Milwaukee for its Great Circus Parade.

  Through October, all exhibit building are open; admission is $5, $2.50 for children 5–12.

  Only the Irvin Feld Exhibit Hall & Visitor Center is open in winter; admission is $3.25 and $1.75. (608) 356-0800 or (608) 356-8341.

- **Wisconsin Dells:** It's 15 miles north. For information on water parks, boat tours and resorts, call (800) 223-3557.

- **Accommodations:** There are many family motels; call the Baraboo Chamber of Commerce for a list. Devil's Lake State Park, three miles south of Baraboo, has 415 campsites. (608) 356-8301.

- **Restaurants:** Culver's Frozen Custard and Butter Burgers, a Wisconsin chain started in nearby Sauk City, is high-quality fast food, served in a pleasant restaurant setting. It's on Highway 33 on the border with West Baraboo.

- **Nightlife:** The ornate Al Ringling Theatre downtown, built in 1915 as a model of the opera house at Versailles, presents movies, local theater and dance and touring shows. (608) 356-8864.

- **Information:** Baraboo Chamber of Commerce, (800) BARABOO.

Train Excursions
Return of a beloved anachronism

Three flushed men in pinstriped overalls worked furiously, shoveling coal atop the locomotive as acrid smoke filled the air around the 1916 brick depot in Osceola, Wisconsin. Suddenly, with a burst of steam, a blast of the whistle and a ringing bell, it headed off down the tracks, soon to return on the other side and be coupled onto three passenger cars.

Steam locomotives are noisy, smelly and inefficient; that's why they've been commercially extinct for a quarter of a century. But the old engines are marvelously evocative, and those who love them are legion.

In many areas, rail museums and private operators once again are running steam- and diesel-powered trains, to the immense joy of aficionados.

"This is the most fascinating machine ever made," a father reverently told his toddler daughter on the Osceola platform, as he watched for the return of the 1907 steam locomotive.

In Osceola, where steam trains run to Dresser and back occasionally through the summer, the volunteers look like museum pieces themselves. When we rode, the engineman was in goggles and red bandana and the fireman in a baggy shop cap. Even the grime is authentic. "It's fun to see someone with soot on his face," said Wes Carlson, one of many Minnesota Transportation Museum volunteers along for the ride.

As we clacked across the bridge over Osceola and through and a corridor of trees, flecks of cinders flew through the window into my lap. The breathy growl of the whistle came again and again. Past cornfields and Christmas-tree farms, past the Trap Rock Inn and Solid Rock Foursquare Church we rumbled to Dresser, which ships out trap rock, used in road construction, on this line during the week.

There, everyone got off the train and watched as the locomotive uncoupled and steamed away and around. When it returned, a blast of white steam bathed our knees, and a prolonged whistle blast had children cowering, then fleeing back onto the train.

The Osceola & St. Croix Valley Railway also runs diesel-engine trips to Dresser and Marine on St. Croix.

In North Freedom, Wisconsin, the Mid-Continent Railway Museum runs four steam trains a day out of a restored 1894 depot whose sidings are cluttered with old trains waiting to be restored.

As we waited on the platform one day in June, a locomotive pulled into the depot with plumes of steam and black smoke. "Now that's a train!" cried a teen-aged boy.

This engine has a heck of a toot, a raw, impatient blast that speaks of frontiers to settle and forests to clear. It was built in 1912 as an oil burner for the Saginaw Lumber Co., which didn't want coal cinders sparking fires in its yards, and hauled timber in Washington state.

Now, it hauls tourists and school groups five miles through scrub forest and the old mining town of La Rue, today just a tavern with a few ponies grazing in the back yard. At the end of the line, we and all the other passengers climbed up a platform to look inside the engine; then we headed back.

In its vast coach shed, the museum stores restored cars: a bright-red, 1925 Great Northern caboose, with a "See America First" logo; a 1906 snow-plow engine; a cafe-parlor car from 1884. It's all that's left of a bygone era.

❀ TRIP TIPS: Train Excursions

- The Osceola & St. Croix Valley Railway out of Osceola, Wis., runs on weekends from Memorial Day through October; 45-minute diesel trips to Dresser, $7 for adults, $3 for children 5–15, $20 for two adults and two to five children, and 1 1/2-hour trips to Marine on St. Croix, $10 adults, $6 children, $30 families. Steam trains to Dresser run some weekends. Call (612) 228-0263.

- The Mid-Continent Railway in North Freedom, Wis., eight miles west of Baraboo, offers hourlong steam-train trips daily from mid-May through Labor Day and weekends until the third weekend of October, plus a Santa Express Thanksgiving weekend and a snow train the third weekend of February. Fare is $8 adults, $4.50 children, $22 family. First-class trips, $18.50, and brunch and dinner trips, $45, also are scheduled. Call (608) 522-4261.

- The Kettle Moraine Steam Train in North Lake, Wis., 30 miles northwest of Milwaukee, runs 45-minute trips Sundays from the first Sunday of June through mid-October. Fare is $7 adults, $3.50 children 3–11. Call (414) 782-8074.

In Duluth, the North Shore Scenic Railroad offers diesel-engine excursions through town and to Two Harbors from May through October; call (218) 722-1273.

Also in Duluth, the Lake Superior & Mississippi Railroad runs 90-minute diesel-engine trips along the St. Louis River at 11 A.M. and 2 P.M. Saturdays and Sundays from June 15 through Labor Day. The starting point is opposite the Lake Superior Zoo. Fares are $6, $4 for children 12 and under. Call (218) 624-7549 (during the season) or (218) 727-0687.

Fur-Trade Rendezvous
The colorful life of a voyageur

Long before the pioneers plodded into the Midwest behind oxen and carts, a far more colorful breed operated here.

They were the voyageurs, thousands of them, uneducated men recruited from villages along the St. Lawrence River to paddle into the continent's interior, propelling birchbark canoes loaded with the goods that the company traders would give Indians in return for animal pelts.

The voyageurs wore floppy red hats and sashes, subsisted on quarts of dried peas and bacon grease, belted out French ditties to relieve the tedium and worked like oxen before collapsing for the night under a canoe turned on its side.

They were, in fact, beasts of burden, known for performing prodigious feats of strength and endurance without complaint. They didn't trap and they didn't trade, nor did they have any hope of doing so—the vast fortunes made from selling the furs of otter, beaver, mink and muskrat in Europe went to the gentlemen bourgeois.

But the voyageurs lived with a magnificent machismo that is compelling today.

"They enjoyed the thrill of challenging the elements and facing the unknown," says Jack Adams, a member of Albert Lea's

Big Island Voyageurs, a re-enactment group. "If they were faint of heart, they didn't last very long."

And, though they were virtually indentured servants, they also were the first to blaze trails, name geographical landmarks and settle cities. They didn't live long, being often felled by back injuries and hernias, but they lived lustily—and at no time more than at rendezvous, where, Adams says, "they partied, drank and made up for the time out on the river."

Rendezvous was when the bourgeois did his business and the voyageurs could relax. They sang, danced and—boasting being an important voyageur attribute—competed to see who could paddle fastest, carry the heaviest pack and throw a hatchet the hardest.

Today, fur-trade rendezvous still are held on the sites of old posts—Grand Portage, Prairie du Chien, Forts Folle Avoine, Traverse des Sioux—and at many other places where people who have gotten hooked on the era gather, in full costume, to live as the voyageurs did.

One year, my family and I went to one of the larger gatherings, the Big Island Rendezvous outside Albert Lea. On a stage, three pairs of cloggers tapped and trilled to fiddle music. Tall men in fur hats and head-to-toe buckskin—coureurs de bois, or independent trappers—wandered the grounds, chewing on roasted turkey legs. Traders sold bone chokers, bobcat tails, leggings—everything a re-enactor needs.

But the real fun was at the voyageurs camp near the lake. There, two men, called by the names of their posts, were teetering on wood blocks, playing a tug-of-war game called Cat and Mouse and insulting each other and themselves with relish.

"It is said to be a voyageur you must be as strong as an ox and very nearly as smart," shouted Rainy Lake just before Fond du Lac yanked him off his block. "Ah, mon Dieu!"

Then a fiddler and concertina player struck up a tune for a paddle dance, in which a lady chooses between two partners by handing a canoe paddle to the loser, then whirls down the lines of men and women. I picked a voyageur in a bandana and a little dark mustache who rewarded me with a courtly bow and a "Merci, mademoiselle" after our spin down the line.

At the black-powder shoot, muskets were going off with sharp booms amid puffs of smoke. My husband tried the 'hawk throw, aiming for a target propped on a log easel.

Farther on, a woman in shawl and voluminous skirts tended a kettle of chicken-rice soup, steaming over an open fire. A man in a plumed tricorner hat discussed birchbark-canoe construction as three other men listened raptly.

Back near traders' row, storyteller Karen Randall was telling a folk tale about poor Pierre the ox-cart driver. After she finished, we bought a children's bow-and-arrow for $5 and looked for the popcorn that everyone else seemed to be eating.

"I don't know whether it's got snake spit in it or what, but it sure is good," remarked the man who directed us to the big bronze cauldron into which a woman was stirring "a little secret sauce."

Today, says Albert Lea bourgeois Perry Vining, a family can go to a rendezvous every weekend, and some do.

"A lot of people do this instead of golfing or fishing," he says. "People get the bug."

✪ TRIP TIPS: Fur-trader rendezvous

Daily admission fees are about $5. Prairie du Chien's is free and is the largest, with 20,000 spectators daily and 4,000 participants.

- Bloody Lake Rendezvous, Woodford, Wisconsin, southwest of Madison; (608) 966-3728. First weekend in May.
- White Blossoms-Black Powder Festival in Gays Mills, Wisconsin, south of La Crosse; (608) 735-4341. Mother's Day weekend.
- Crossroads Rendezvous, Saukville, Wisconsin, north of Milwaukee; (414) 284-6742. Third weekend of May.
- Eagle Creek Rendezvous, Murphy's Landing in Shakopee, Minnesota; (612) 445-6901. Memorial Day weekend.
- Fur Trade Rendezvous, Fort Atkinson, Wisconsin, southeast of Madison; (414) 563-3210. First weekend in June.
- Fort Ridgely Rendezvous, Fort Ridgely State Park west of New Ulm, Minnesota; (507) 426-7840. Usually second weekend of June.
- Prairie Villa Rendezvous, Prairie du Chien, Wisconsin; (800) 732-1673. Father's Day weekend.
- Mille Lacs History Festival and Rendezvous outside Isle, Minnesota. Last weekend of June. (320) 676-3945 (Memorial Day–Labor Day).
- Great Rendezvous, Old Fort William, Thunder Bay, Ontario. Ten days starting the second weekend of July at the world's largest reconstructed fur-trade post. (807) 577-8461, (800) 667-8386.

- Great Forts Folle Avoine Rendezvous, Danbury, Wisconsin, east of Hinckley, Minnesota; (715) 866-8890, (715) 349-2219. Third weekend in July.
- Original Midwest National Rendezvous, White Oak Fur Post, Deer River, Minnesota; (218) 246-9393. Last weekend in July and first weekend of August.
- Grand Portage Rendezvous, Grand Portage, Minnesota; (218) 387-2788. Second weekend in August. The Grand Portage Pow-wow is held at the same time.
- Fur Trade Rendezvous, Fort Snelling in the Twin Cities; (612) 726-1171. Labor Day weekend.
- Traverse des Sioux Rendezvous, St. Peter, Minnesota; (507) 931-2160, (507) 373-9209. Weekend after Labor Day.
- Wild Rice Rendezvous, North West Company Fur Post, Pine City, Minnesota. Mid-September. Owned by the Minnesota Historical Society, it's on the site of an 1804–05 camp built by Canadian traders and is open May through Labor Day. Costumed guides portray voyageurs, traders and the Ojibwe men and women who helped them; (320) 629-6356, (612) 296-6126.
- Two River Rendezvous, Bloomington, Minnesota; (612) 374-2440. Third weekend in September.
- Big Island Rendezvous, Albert Lea, Minnesota; (800) 658-2526. First full weekend in October.

11 HISTORIC SITES

Living History
In Forestville, the summer of 1899

The young man behind the counter in the country store is scandalized.

"I can't help but notice you're wearing your drawers," he admonishes, averting his eyes from our baggy shorts. "Around here, we like a lady to cover her knees and ankles." Then he shows us a bolt of calico, 5 cents a yard, that he thinks we might like to make into a dress, preferably as soon as possible.

Charles Ball lives amid the fashions and mores of 1899, and so, for an afternoon, did my daughter and I. Meighen Store, where Ball works, is in Forestville, once a frontier trade center, now a ghost town. Except now, the ghosts have come back to life.

As we cross a small steel bridge and approach the town, a man in soft hat and vest rises from a barrel-top checkerboard to greet us. It's Ball, a laborer for Thomas Meighen, son of the town founder and the man who owns the store and the brick home, wagon barn, granary and animal barn near it.

After Ball waits on us in the store, we go next door, where 28-year-old Mary Meighen, Thomas' bride, welcomes us into her parlor and tells us of her restlessness in the country—she's a city girl, from Preston, and her husband often is away at meetings of the Populist Party.

Then she leads us into the kitchen, where she is putting up strawberry jam. We watch her put another piece of wood into the big iron stove and, her face flushed by the heat, pour paraffin onto the jam. She slips a sugar cookie to my daughter before answering a tinkling bell: More guests await her at the front door.

We go out the back door and are immediately taken up by laborer Charlie Martin, who shows us a barn emptied of animals—"Mr. Meighen heard the tax assessor was coming, so he took them to some property he owns in the next township"—

and lets my daughter gather three eggs from the chicken coop. In the wagon barn, he puts her and two other kids to work sawing logs with a bucksaw.

Then Martin, a.k.a. Gene Hokanson of Chatfield, breaks character and explains that, in 1899, Forestville already was dying. It was founded in 1853 and flourished until it was bypassed by the railroad in 1868. When people started leaving, Thomas Meighen (pronounced MEE'an) bought up the surrounding land and buildings and turned it into a company town. In 1902, rural delivery was started, and neighboring farmers no longer had to go to the store to pick up mail. The Meighens moved to Preston and closed the store in 1910.

But Thomas Meighen didn't sell off the inventory of the store or barns; he wanted Forestville to be part of a state park. His daughter, Margaret, made sure the state was able to buy it, and Forestville State Park opened in 1968. In 1990, the Minnesota Historical Society took over the town, wrote a social history from the voluminous documents Meighen left behind and, in 1992, opened Historic Forestville with interpreters playing the part of residents.

The site is one of five run by the Minnesota Historical Society that use the technique. Two sites in northern Minnesota also use costumed interpreters, as do Fort Snelling in the Twin Cities, the Oliver Kelley Farm near Elk River and the private Murphy's Landing near Shakopee.

At the Forest History Center near Grand Rapids, there are three historical zones: a 1900 logging camp; a moored Mississippi River wanigan, the barge that served as headquarters during a 1901 log drive; and a 1934 forest-service patrolman's cabin. Here, lumberjacks, blacksmiths, clerks, cooks and the lonely patrolman tell their stories and that of the forest around them.

At the North West Company Fur Post, a reconstructed post on the original site near Pine City, the year is 1804. John Sayer is in charge of eight voyageurs and a clerk, plus the Ojibwe women Nokomis and Benakwe, who can be seen flushing and dressing the hides their husbands bring in—actually, road kill or confiscated hides from the DNR.

Visitors may taste the day's ration of a quart of hominy seasoned with an ounce of bear grease or deer tallow. Food is important here: Each voyageur also is allotted eight pounds of meat per day—venison, bear, beaver—purchased from an Ojibwe hunter.

"Interpreting is really an art," says site manager Patrick Schifferdecker, who plays guide-interpreter Francois Boucher. "You're trying to get people to temporarily suspend disbelief that you actually are in 1804."

At Forestville, visitors leave the 1990s at the parking lot, intentionally put at a distance. By the time they arrive at the town, the years have fallen away. The buzz of insects in the nearby woods is the loudest noise; often, horses and their riders canter by, slowing to get a look at the town from the past.

It's a frontier Brigadoon. Leave it, and it disappears into the mists of history—until next time.

✪ TRIP TIPS: Minnesota living-history sites

- Historic Forestville is in Forestville State Park near Preston. It's open Tuesdays–Sundays, Memorial Day through Labor Day, and weekends through early October. A $4 state-park sticker is required. Call (507) 765-2785.

- The Forest History Center is near highways 169 and 2 southwest of Grand Rapids. Interpretations are given daily from Memorial Day through Oct. 15; the museum is open weekdays in the winter, when two miles of trails are groomed for skiing. Among many events are the Woodcrafts Festival, second or third weekend in July, and Christmas in a 1900 Logging Camp, second weekend in December. Admission is $4 adults, $2 children ages 6–15. Call (218) 327-4482.

- The Northwest Company Fur Post is on Highway 7 just west of Pine City. After Labor Day, it closes until May 1 except for special events, including its Wild Rice Rendezvous in September. Free admission. Call (612) 629-6356 or, in the winter, (612) 296-6126.

Fire Museum

In Hinckley, an 1894 inferno

On a September day little more than a century ago, Hinckley, Minnesota, was hell on earth.

Throughout the summer of 1894, less than two inches of rain fell. Small fires smoldered in the Minnesota's timberlands, many started when hot cinders from trains landed in tinder-dry slashings—the crowns, stumps and branches left behind by logging crews.

On September 1, breezes fanned small fires near Mission Creek and Pokegama, villages south of Hinckley. They joined, and the flames, breaking through a thick layer of warm air, were turned into a fiery cyclone by cool air traveling down from above.

It quickly moved north toward Hinckley, where it became a 4½-mile-high wall of fire. The air in its path became so hot buildings seemed to melt, not burn. Fireballs appeared out of nowhere, flying through the air.

By 6 P.M. that day, six towns, including Hinckley and Sandstone, had been destroyed. At least 418 people were dead. "TWO MINNESOTA TOWNS UTTERLY DESTROYED BY FIRE," read the front page of the next day's *New York Times*. "GREAT FOREST FIRES IN AMERICA" read the first of five days' worth of front-page coverage in the *London Times*.

Today, the tales of heroism and tragedy told at the Hinckley Fire Museum are just as gripping as they were 100 years ago.

"My grandfather used to tell me about the Hinckley Fire when I was a young girl growing up in Minneapolis," says Jeanne Coffey, director of the museum. "It was an intriguing thing to him."

Among the heroes were St. Paul & Duluth engineer Jim Root, his fireman, John McGowan, and porter, John Blair, who arrived on a train from the north just as the fire reached Hinckley from the south. With an extra load of panicked townspeople, they backed up the flaming train to Skunk Lake, where nearly 300 people huddled in 18 inches of mud and slime as the fire passed over them. Today, bicyclists pass Skunk Lake on the old rail bed, now part of Willard Munger State Trail.

The fire sites begin just east of Tobie's along Fire Monument

Road. On the north side of the road is Memorial Cemetery, where a 51-foot granite monument rises above four long trenches that contain the remains of 248 victims. Back toward town, the road ends in the juncture of two rail lines. Along one is Memorial Park, site of a gravel pit in which 100 people huddled in water and were saved.

Three blocks north along the other line is the St. Paul and Duluth Depot, rebuilt soon after the original burned. Now it's the museum, visited by 20,000 people each year. There, the story is graphically told.

A movie in the old freight room, smelling of aged planks, explains how "promiscuous" logging and extraordinarily hot, dry weather led to the destruction of "The Town Built From Wood," which had 1,200 to 1,500 residents before the fire. The narrative is broken by accounts from survivors.

In the old telegrapher's room, a plaster likeness of 25-year-old Thomas Dunn sits awaiting Root's train from Duluth, on which members of Dunn's family were traveling. A tape records his last message: "I think I've stayed too long."

Pathos is unavoidable. Among the grisliest of the museum's exhibits is the coroner's death list, which lists the dead by number. Nos. 314–415 are "unknown," including No. 326: "Male, found in lumber yard. Only jack knife, watch and buttons left. Not enough found to be buried."

Heroism and venality, miracles and wretched bad luck. It's all part of the Hinckley story.

"This was a big deal," says Jeanne Coffey. "This was a fire to talk about."

❂ TRIP TIPS: Hinckley

- **Fire Museum:** Open daily May to mid-October. Admission is $3 adults, $1.50 teens, 50 cents children 6–12.
- **Events:** Hinckley Corn and Clover Carnival, weekend after the Fourth of July.
- **Lodgings:** Dakota Lodge B&B is 10 miles east; $58–$110, (320) 384-6052. Also: Days Inn, (800) 325-2525; Gold Pine Motor Inn, (800) 798-6027; Grand Casino RV Resort, (800) 995-GRAND; Holiday Inn Express, (800) HOLIDAY; Tobie's Motor Lodge, (320) 384-7451.
- **Information:** (320) 384-0126, (320) 384-7338.

Caddie Woodlawn Country
Traces of a remarkable childhood

In 1864, a remarkable 11-year-old named Caddie Woodhouse was living a childhood idyll in the wilderness of western Wisconsin, gathering wild grapes and hazelnuts in the woods, dodging rattlesnakes and fording the Menomonie River on tiptoe to watch her Santee Dakota friends make birchbark canoes.

She was the great-granddaughter of an English lord, her stories went, and she could have been the daughter of one if her father had not turned down the title and ancestral manor in favor of his own wood-frame house and 160 acres near Dunnville. She had a resourceful head and a loyal heart, and she loved to hear and tell stories.

Those tales were set to paper in 1935 by one of Caddie's granddaughters, Carol Ryrie Brink, and they became the Newbery-winning children's classic *Caddie Woodlawn*.

Caddie's house still exists on the original homestead, eight miles south of Menomonie. It's a handsome cottage with gray shakes and a bay window—a palace, if you're expecting the dugouts and shanties of Laura Ingalls Wilder's childhood. The house is part of what the Dunn County Historical Society calls Caddie Woodlawn Country, an early logging center. It's farmland now but has an untamed face, due to the rolling topography and the path cut by the Red Cedar River, once the Menomonie.

Which is to say, there's room to imagine. When we visited one bright Sunday in April, my young daughter, a third-generation fan of Caddie, immediately caught her heroine's spirit. Tearing around the grounds, and venturing a few steps into the woods behind the house, she found a white feather and came back brandishing it, shouting, "This is the secret treasure of Caddie Woodlawn! Think it is?"

We started our trip in the college town of Menomonie, with a look at Mabel Tainter Memorial Theater, a building with an ornately detailed sandstone facade and jewel-box interior. It was built in 1890 by Andrew Tainter, one of the founders of Knapp, Stout Co., the largest lumbering company in the world at the time, in memory of his 19-year-old daughter. Along with a full slate of theater and concerts, the Tainter occasionally presents a stage version of *Caddie Woodlawn* written by Carol Ryrie Brink.

In Riverside Park, just across the Highway 29 bridge, Red Cedar Outfitters was doing a brisk business as parties of bicyclists set out on the 14½-mile Red Cedar State Trail, which follows the old rail bed along the west bank of the Red Cedar to Downsville, where it crosses to the east bank.

Judging from the bicycle rack outside the Creamery in Downsville, many of the cyclists ended up there, as we did, for its renowned Sunday brunch. We loaded our plates with scones, fresh fruit, shrimp fettuccine, lamb goulash; our children plowed through an omelet, corn-bread pancakes, sausage patties, a good deal of watermelon and big bowls of Haagen-Dazs before running onto the back lawn to harass the three resident hounds, dozing in the sun.

On Highway C in Downsville is the boxy sandstone Empire in Pine Museum, which commemorates the lumbering era, of which Caddie's father, millwright John Woodhouse, was a part. Down the street, an antiques shop occupies the original building of the Knapp Stout Co. Store, established by the giant lumber company in 1857, the year the Woodhouse family arrived from Boston.

Two miles down Highway 25 is the Caddie Woodlawn Memorial Park, a pleasant, pine-shaded area that contains the family's house, a sandstone shelter with two hearths, picnic tables, a water pump and a smokehouse. Visitors to the house can walk through the rooms; up the stairs to the attic, where Caddie accidentally started her career mending clocks; and onto the back porch, where the oldest among the seven children churned butter in the summer.

Our daughter ran to the smokehouse, tried the door and ran back, excited: "Caddie put a stick in the door of the little house," she said.

Then we started following a map of the area as it was in 1864, drawn by Dunn County historian John Russell. Driving down County Road Y, we could see a wooded ridge, around which Caddie and her brothers and sisters took a short cut to the schoolhouse on the other side, run only in winter and summer because the Dunnville kids had to share a teacher with the kids in Durand. Caddie's school isn't there, but the 1908 brick schoolhouse that replaced it, now a private residence, is.

Around the trestle bridge across the Red Cedar, a dozen people were fishing from a makeshift campground. "Don't you ever try to walk across a river," my husband told our daughter, thinking of the many times Caddie, who couldn't swim, crossed the river with her clothes on her head.

Across the bridge is the Red Cedar Trail, which then runs into the Dunnville Wildlife Area and to the Chippewa River. There, it connects with the Chippewa River Trail, which runs another 20 miles into Eau Claire.

We walked up the shaded trail for a stretch, thinking of the steamer that docked here, bringing mail, supplies and news of the Civil War to the Woodhouses, who could hear its whistle from their farm.

Two years after the year chronicled in *Caddie Woodlawn,* the steamer took Caddie and her family south to St. Louis. Caddie, who lived to be 86, eventually ended up in Idaho, where her skill at telling a story made her beloved by her grandchildren and, through one of them, by children throughout the world.

❂ TRIP TIPS: Caddie Woodlawn Country

- **Getting around:** For a copy of the Caddie Woodlawn Country brochure, call the Menomonie Area Chamber of Commerce, (800) 283-1862, which also can supply other information.
- **Food and lodgings:** The Creamery restaurant, (715) 664-8354, is open for lunch and dinner Tuesdays–Sundays, April through New Year's. The four rooms rent for $100–$130; for weekends; book well in advance.
- **Mabel Tainter Memorial Theater:** It presents theater, concerts, children's plays and even art fairs all year. Tours are given at 1, 2, 3 and 4 P.M. daily year-round, $3; mini-tours are $1.50. For a schedule of events, call (715) 235-9726; for tickets, call (715) 235-0001.
- **Rentals:** Red Cedar Outfitters, (715) 235-5431, rents bicycles, canoes and tubes and provides a shuttle service. A daily state trail pass costs $3; nual pass costs $10.

Canterbury Inn

On the road to heaven in Madison

In Geoffrey Chaucer's 14th century work *Canterbury Tales,* the owner of an inn outside London issues a challenge to 29 pilgrims headed for the shrine of St. Thomas à Becket, the archbishop of Canterbury murdered for opposing Henry II. The pilgrim who tells the best tale on the journey wins a free dinner.

Note the key elements: Good stories. Good food and drink. A good night's sleep. That's why Madison's Canterbury Inn, part of a bookstore and coffeehouse, couldn't be more aptly named.

At this inn, Petrarch and Boccaccio become Alice Walker and John Irving; tankards of mead become cappuccino and cafe latte. And all the traveler's needs are met.

I figured the inn was worth a pilgrimage. What better place to hole up for a winter weekend than a small inn built above 60,000 books? The evening I chose, an Illinois author would be reading from his new novel. A duo would perform Irish folk music on hammered dulcimer and acoustic guitar. Wine and cheese would be served.

No reason to go anywhere. But one of the other charms of the Canterbury Inn is that it's a few doors off State Street, the five-block stretch of shops, cafes and museums between the gold-domed state Capitol and the University of Wisconsin.

As I walked along it on a waning afternoon in November, I fell in behind a young woman with long green hair and army boots. The odors of falafel, Indian cotton and Kona roast hung in the crisp air; in the distance, a marching band began to play. At a hat shop, a voluble young clerk in wire rims filled me in on the Badgers' football fortunes.

If you didn't already know, State Street tells you: This is a College Town. Nearer the Capitol, the street scene shifted. Shoppers were streaming into the Holiday Art Fair in the Civic

Center, which also houses an art center and performing space for theater, dance, opera and music. At Deb & Lola's, waiters were bent over linen-covered tables, lighting candles.

Back at the Canterbury Inn, fresh pineapple, kiwi, grapes, oranges and grapefruit had been set out with cheese, crackers and wine in the parlor. With plate and glass, I settled into a wingback chair and read the *Isthmus,* a weekly paper named for the narrow strip of land between lakes Mendota and Monona, through which State Street runs.

To get to the parlor, guests go through a trompe l'oeil door—well, the door is real, but the scene painted upon it is trickery—portraying heavy wood beams with an arched slot looking into a medieval tavern. Doors to the six rooms are painted with depictions of their namesakes—Clerk, Knight, Wife of Bath—and inside the rooms are murals depicting the tale each told, framed by trompe l'oeil columns.

My room was the simplest—no Jacuzzi, kitchen, sitting room or skylight—but it did have lovely fresh flowers and a CD player. I put on Haydn's piano trios and inspected my private library—Alice Munro, Primo Levi and Harriet Doerr—and stash of snacks—chocolate-chip bars, juice, sodas.

Downstairs, the author of the day, Reginald Gibbons, had appeared to read a chapter from his first novel, *Sweetbitter,* a love story set in turn-of-the-century Texas. Only four of us showed up, but Gibbons was unruffled; after he read, we all chatted in the cafe over coffee, provided on the house.

Then the husband-and-wife duo Molly and the Tinker got on stage and began to pull waves of belly laughs out of a packed cafe with bawdy one-liners, but also lovely ballads. From my table, where I sat eating Greek salad and lemon-custard tart, I watched, awestruck, as Molly's hands flew over the dulcimer: "musical arrangements by Mario Andretti," her husband noted.

In the morning, the croissants, fruit and freshly squeezed orange juice I had ordered the night before arrived on the dot, with the *New York Times.* After I had descended to the bookstore and spent the $10 gift certificate that comes with each room, it was time to go, but I stalled by leafing through the guest book. The comments were wackier than they usually are in these books; after all, these guests are the type who read Chaucer.

But aside from the bon mots, there was a consensus: The Canterbury is an inn from heaven. To that I say, amen.

✪ TRIP TIPS: Canterbury Inn

- **Rates:** Clerk's room, $117–$145; Reeve's, $127–$155; Knight's, $182–$210; Miller's and Wife of Bath's, $202–$230; Merchant's, $237–$255. On football weekends and holidays, rates are $20 more. (800) 838-3850.
- **Events:** The Civic Center, 211 State St., is the venue for international artists and Broadway shows as well as the local symphony, opera and theater and dance troupes. For tickets, call (608) 266-9055; for a list of events, call (608) 266-6550.
- **Information:** Greater Madison Convention & Visitors Bureau, (800) 373-6376.

Culinary Pilgrimages
Fine dining at inns

Candlelight from a dozen iron sconces flickered on knotty-pine walls and gilt mirrors. On a table set for 20, shadows slid along the silver and crystal, waxing and waning with the flames out of the stone fireplace.

On this night, the Outing Lodge at Pine Point near Stillwater, Minnesota, had become a temple of gastronomy.

It's not every day I sit down to a place setting that's flanked by five forks, four knives, two spoons and five glasses. But excess was required—this was Babette's Feast, a re-creation of the meal served in the Oscar-winning Danish film of the same name. In the 1987 film, a Parisian chef, living as a political refugee within an ascetic religious community in Denmark, wins 10,000 francs in a lottery and cuts loose 14 years of suppressed creativity by preparing dinner for her hosts and their dour friends.

Nobody was dour on this night. Proprietor Lee Gohlike, a cherubic man in a red bow tie, presided over a gathering that was more like a dinner party.

Guests converged on the table from the front room, where they'd been sipping drinks before an enormous hearth, and from the darkened library, where they'd been watching Babette turn a cage of burbling quail, a snapping turtle and several wheelbarrows of other goods into a repast for the gods.

As soon as we sat down, tureens of turtle consomme with veal quenelles appeared, along with amontillado sherry. Blinis with Danish caviar, crème fraiche and grated lemon came next, with Chase-Limogère Champagne.

Quail in a puff-pastry "sarcophagus" was up next; my husband leaned over and whispered, "If they give me a little bird with its head still on, I don't know what I'll say." In the movie, the quail's head is snapped off and the brains lustily sucked out, but not here: "At first, we tried to get people to put a coin near their plate—heads or tails—to show whether they wanted it," Gohlike said with a smile, "but even so, people didn't like to see others sucking the brains out of the head."

Glasses were filled and refilled with velvety Nuits-Saint-Georges burgundy with a heady aroma. A salad with walnut vinaigrette was served, followed by a selection of blue cheeses, a rich baba au rhum and, finally, plates of papaya, pomegranate, mango and tangerine. I gave my snifter of cognac to my husband, who, by then, just like the people in the movie, was smiling beatifically.

Gohlike has been offering Babette's Feast since 1988 at his Outing Lodge, an imposing, 1923 brick building that was an abandoned nursing home when he bought and renovated it.

Today, it is a B&B that is remarkable for its lovely grounds and location along the Gateway State Trail out of St. Paul. Trails wind through the inn's 25 acres and the 325 acres in adjoining Pine Point Park; in the winter, the trails are groomed for cross-country skiing.

Gohlike has patterned his country inn after those in Europe, where the culinary pilgrimage is a tradition. There, the best country restaurants have a few rooms they rent to those who are in too much of a gourmet swoon to go anywhere but upstairs.

In Europe, people use Michelin guides to eat their way from one three-star restaurant to the next. Here, word of mouth keeps the good inns going. They provide a one-stop weekend: Check in, spend the evening over a meal and stagger off to sleep.

At the Outing Lodge, Babette's Feast is held at least twice a year, $89 per person, in addition to an English Christmas dinner, $68, Russian New Year's, $88, and two in which the lib-

eral amounts of alcohol are not included, Valentine's, $48,
and St. Patrick's Day, $34. There's also open dining, but call
ahead. Twelve rooms cost $85–$190. Call (612) 439-9747.

✪ TRIP TIPS: Culinary Pilgrimages

Here are a few other candidates for weekend dining:

- Old Rittenhouse Inn, Bayfield, Wisconsin. (715) 779-5111. 20
  rooms, $99–$199, among three Victorian houses. A six-course
  dinner of seasonal specialties costs $37.50. Harvest, wassail
  and Valentine's dinner concerts are $40.
- Mrs. B's, Lanesboro, Minnesota. (800) 657-4710, (507) 467-2154.
  Circa 1870 B&B with 10 rooms, $50–$95. Five-course meal of
  seasonal specialties, $23, Wednesday–Sunday.
- Lumber Baron's Hotel, Stillwater, Minnesota. (612) 439-6000.
  Renovated 1890 brick building, dressed to the nines in Victoriana. Forty-two suites and rooms, $139–$229. Five-course traditional Victorian dinner, $32; entrees, $14–$22.
- Schumacher's New Prague Hotel, New Prague, Minnesota. (612)
  758-2133. European-style inn with 11 rooms, $107–$165. German and Bohemian entrees, $20–$25 a la carte.
- Covington Inn B&B, St. Paul, Minnesota. (612) 292-1411. 1946
  towboat on the Mississippi, moored across from downtown.
  Four rooms, $95–$180. Seasonal specialties and vegetarian
  fare, $9–$15 a la carte.

Canoe Bay
Luxury in the woods

Imagine a Wisconsin lake resort filled with fresh flowers,
stained glass, original art and Prairie-style furniture in
which to sit while listening to a CD chosen from the resort's library. Oh, and a hot breakfast delivered in a basket each
morning. It's not really the north woods—but then, who cares?

Besides, the term "Wisconsin lake resort," with its conno-
tation of jet-skis, reeking fish houses and shrieking children,
makes proprietor Dan Dobrowolski shudder.

"I wish someone could tell me what we are—somewhere between resort, B&B and country inn," he says. "Our big thing is luxury, privacy and peace."

Dobrowolski abandoned a career as a television meteorologist in Chicago—don't get him started on the quality of TV news shows—to lead a more civilized life. To do that, he created Canoe Bay Inn and Cottages on an old Seventh Day Adventist retreat across the lake from his grandfather's farm near Chetek, in west-central Wisconsin.

Dobrowolski and his wife, Lisa, "blew the buildings apart," rebuilt them in the spirit of Frank Lloyd Wright and filled them with exquisite art and furniture commissioned from local craftsmen.

"We went down the list and asked ourselves, 'What do we want?' and we hoped people would be like us," says Dobrowolski, who calls himself "obsessed with having something very unique in every way." They opened the resort in 1993.

When I was there one January, a gas fire glowed in the 30-foot fieldstone fireplace, Mozart was playing softly, and Lisa Dobrowolski was gliding around filling bowls with M&Ms and chocolate-chip cookies. In one of the outlying cottages, Pat and Karin Mascia of Roseville were getting ready to ski on the resort's small private lake.

"We've been to a lot of places, and this one goes right to the top of the list now," Pat Mascia said.

With the breakfast baskets come the day's weather forecast, various notes and the evening menu—say, squash soup, grilled beef tenderloin with cranberry bearnaise and Linzertorte, $60 per couple, served in a glass-enclosed lakeside dining room.

"People come because it's a great place, and then they'd like to have some great food, so we had to hire a chef," Dan Dobrowolski says, with a sigh at his own punctiliousness. "It's godawful expensive."

It was a gamble to build such a luxurious resort in an area of Wisconsin better known for its supper clubs and mom-and-pop resorts. But Dobrowolski had faith in his vision.

"As much as I was optimistic and kept up a good face, I had my doubts, too," says Dobrowolski. "But there's a market of people who want the goods."

✪ TRIP TIPS: Canoe Bay

- **Getting there:** It's nine miles east of Chetek, Wisconsin.
- **Rates:** Four inn rooms, $160–$180; three lodge rooms, $135–$165; four rooms in two cottages, $175–$205; and the Dream Cottage, $245. Two-night minimum on weekends; midweek discount. All rooms have whirlpools, VCRs, CD players and small refrigerators; some have a fireplace. Smoke-free; no children.
- **Sports:** Use of cross-country skis, canoes and rowboats are included, as well as fees at a nearby golf course.
- **Information:** (800) 568-1995, (715) 924-4594.

Fanny Hill
A sweet inn in Eau Claire

On a hill high above Eau Claire, Wisconsin, is an inn with a name that's rather suggestive for this area, the name of a fictional London prostitute whose memoirs have titillated readers since 1749, when they were published, right up to 1966, when a landmark U.S. Supreme Court censorship case gave the lady new notoriety.

Fanny Hill definitely was naughty. But her namesake, the Fanny Hill Inn & Dinner Theatre, is squeaky-clean, as sweet and mild as the teddy bears that, in Easter pinafores or Santa suits according to season, sit in spare nooks and crannies.

However, love *is* in the air.

"Oh, look, honey," cooed a young woman to her husband, as they stood, arms clasped around each other's waists, looking over a velvet rope into one of the inn's rooms. "That's the room we had for our anniversary *last* year."

Valentine's Day is a big event at the inn, but one-stop romance is cultivated all year. In the wood-beamed restaurant, floor-to-ceiling windows draped with lace give guests a spectacular view of the city and a broad stretch of the Chippewa River.

In the theater, plays tend to be the old standards everyone likes. In the rooms, double whirlpools, fireplaces and oversized beds telegraph romance. And in the summer, there are eight acres of formal gardens, dotted with statuary, for hand-in-hand strolls.

But the most surprising thing about Fanny Hill is the quality of its restaurant, which serves dishes—Chilean sea bass with grapefruit beurre blanc, pheasant breast served in a carved acorn squash—not often seen in this area.

This is supper-club country, and, not surprisingly, that's what Fanny Hill used to be; before that, it was a beer hall.

Then owners Dennis and Carol Heyde decided to go Victorian. They painted it peach, with white trim and lots of gables and porches. They enlarged the theater, hired a chef and added bed-and-breakfast rooms. And they decorated, and then decorated some more.

When I stayed there one January, I got to see the end of the year's biggest display, a riot of twinkle lights, garlands, angels and animated Santas that takes a crew of at least eight people from a local boutique two weeks to install. Trees were everywhere; the one in my room, the Lady Anne, was thick with wood-bead garlands, bells and crepe-paper hearts, bows and dolls, all perfectly coordinated in peach and baby-blue.

In fact, the tree looked lifted whole from a country-crafts boutique. Fanny Hill takes a few liberties with its theme, mixing Victoriana with country kitsch. Not to put too fine a point on it, but I doubt many saloons in Queen Victoria's day had a big teddy bear at the end of the bar, slurping from a globe of bubbling green liquid.

So it's not authentic, but certainly cheerful.

When I was there, the play was *Murder at the Howard Johnson's,* in which a woman, her lover and her husband, in various combinations, try to bump each other off over the space of a year. The humor was as broad as the cuckolded husband's midriff—"Where'd you get that gun?" "At Sears; it's their own brand." "A Kenmore?!"—but irresistible.

As were the tortes, cheesecakes and cream puffs whipped out at intermission. Inn guests who did resist could eat the snacks set out for them after the show, cookies, fruit and soda.

Breakfast is included in a night at Fanny Hill; the next morning, I got to see just how lovely the dining room is. It was flooded with sunlight; I gazed at the view and watched cardinals flitting around the feeder as I ate my eggs and bacon. And the service, as it had been at dinner, was impeccable.

There's a ¾-mile trail around the grounds that guests can use in better weather. But I drove down the hill to the 134-acre Carson Park, which includes an oxbow lake of the Chippewa River and is set on a ridge overlooking downtown, and skied a bit on a milelong trail. In the summer, Carson Park is the place to be: There are water-ski shows, minor-league baseball games, rides through the pine woods on an old train, a re-created 1890s logging camp and a year-round museum that includes a turn-of-the-century ice-cream parlor.

The 20-mile Chippewa River State Trail starts nearby in Owen Park, at Lake Street and First Avenue, just shy of the bridge to the faded downtown.

I stopped at Fanny Hill for a moment on my way home. The polar bears were being taken down, and the Easter bunnies were going in. In late summer, a show of teddy bears moves in, followed by scarecrows and 5,000 pumpkins.

But the view, thankfully, always stays the same.

✪ TRIP TIPS: Fanny Hill

- **Getting there:** To get to Fanny Hill from Interstate 94, exit at Highway 12 west of Eau Claire, turn south on Townhall Drive, then east on County Road EE, or Crescent Avenue. The inn is at 3919 Crescent Ave.
- **Restaurant:** Entrees, $9–$27. A Sunday brunch is $11 for adults, $5 children 10 and under.
- **Theater:** Five or six productions per year. Tickets cost $16–$20, $27–$33 with lunch or dinner.
- **Rooms:** Eleven rooms, $79–$165, nine with whirlpools and fireplaces, two with especially panoramic views.
- **Information:** Fanny Hill, (800) 292-8026, (715) 836-8184; Eau Claire Convention and Visitors Bureau, (800) 344-FUNN, (715) 831-2345.

13 THREE SMALL TOWNS

Excelsior
Small-town leisure on Lake Minnetonka

Visiting the Lake Minnetonka village of Excelsior makes me think of an episode of "Twilight Zone," the one in which a beleaguered city office worker, in catnaps on the commuter train, dreams of an idyllic small town from years past. One day, the train's doors open, and there it is, complete with gazebo, laughing children and strolling parents.

Excelsior is like that. In fact, it's practically perfect.

Like that "Twilight Zone" town, it's reached via gantlet— Highway 7, lined the entire way with the commercial outposts of Minneapolis' western suburbs.

But in Excelsior, settled in 1853, the scene changes to 19th century brick storefronts. There's a barber shop, with a rotating pole. A bakery. A pet shop, with bunnies in the window. A bookstore. A movie theater that still shows movies.

At the end of Water Street is the water—Excelsior Bay, in Lake Minnetonka's southwest corner. On a sunny day, when the water is sparkling and the boats at dock are gleaming white, there are few views that are prettier.

Off the small harbor is the Commons, the largest piece of public land on vast Lake Minnetonka. There's a baseball diamond, with bleachers set into a slope; a red, white and blue bandshell; and lots of room for exercising dogs. A century ago, however, it was a promenade for the wealthy.

"Lake Minnetonka probably was the most popular summer resort area west of Saratoga Springs, New York," says Bob Williams, a local resident who has written four historical novels featuring the town. "Excelsior was really the hub. This little dinky town of 500 had 10 trains a day coming into it."

Fleets of passenger steamboats ferried tourists from Excelsior to Wayzata, Tonka Bay and, between 1907 and 1911, to Big Island Park, an amusement park on the island north of town. A new era started in 1925, when Excelsior Amusement Park was built at the tip of the bay, near today's Excelsior Park Tavern. It was famous for its roller coaster and brought in performers from the Andrews Sisters to the Beach Boys. Twin City Rapid Transit Co. streetcars brought in customers from all over the Twin Cities, and it lasted until 1973. On weekends, when the boaters turn out, Excelsior, population 2,600, still is a very busy place. On weekdays, it's quieter.

My daughter and I discovered the town on a warm weekday in September and spent the whole afternoon on the Commons. Then, as now, it was a very pleasant place. Thick grass runs right up to the shore, lined with boulders. Along it geese and ducks swim, watching for anyone who might be bringing crumbs. On a wooded hill behind the bandshell, there are picnic tables and rough steps leading down past wild-rose bushes to a secluded nook along the water.

Farther on are tennis courts, a hill topped by baby swings and then the beach, wrapped around a point. A lifeguard watches swimmers on the side facing Excelsior Bay; on the other side, facing Gideon's Bay, there's a sandy play area with old-fashioned carousel-horse swings and a carved beaver sculpture to match the pelican near the dock.

And one of the original streetcar steamboats, the *Minnehaha,* has been meticulously restored by a squadron of volunteers and has resumed its original duty, ferrying passengers between Excelsior and Wayzata, a lakeshore village with many fine shops and restaurants.

Many people have warm memories of Excelsior, says Bob Williams, who gets big turnouts for his occasional walking tours. The best thing about Excelsior, he says, is that, even though it's surrounded by wealthy suburbs, and has its own share of the well-to-do, it remains a small town.

"It's like a town you'd find 100 miles, 200 miles from Minneapolis," Williams says. "We love it."

○ TRIP TIPS: Excelsior

- **Getting there:** Avoid rush hour.
- **Cruises:** Narrated rides on the *Minnehaha* on summer weekends, an hour each way between Excelsior and Wayzata, cost $8 round-trip for adults, $5 children. Reserve tickets at (612) 474-4801.

- **Events:** Fourth of July, July 4.
  Art on the Lake, second Saturday in June.
  Apple Days, first Saturday following Labor Day.
  Holiday Home Tour, second weekend in December.
- **Nightlife:** The Old Log Theater, across the bay in what now is Greenwood, was founded in 1940 and is the longest continuously running stock theater in the country. It specializes in British farces and Broadway comedy. (612) 474-5951.
- **Accommodations:** The 1887 Christopher Inn, (612) 474-6816, is a bed-and-breakfast that evokes the Victorian era. Its attractively decorated rooms, named for the seven children of proprietors Howard and Joan Johnson, who live next door, range in price from $65 to $130. The inn is on a pine-shaded hill a few blocks from downtown. No unmarried couples.
  The James H. Clark House B&B, an 1858 Italianate on Water Street. Four rooms, $75–$135. (612) 474-0196.
- **Information:** (612) 474-6461.

Hudson

Life along the St. Croix

In summer, many tourists arrive in Hudson, Wisconsin, from the river, wandering up from their moorings on the St. Croix River to stroll down Second Street, looking around and stopping to peer in shop windows.

But when visitors pour into town for the annual Hot Air Affair in early February, they walk quite a bit more briskly.

The river has been Hudson's highway since the first steamboat docked there in 1847. But in winter, leisure traffic moves to the skies above E.P. Rock School, where dozens of hot-air balloons are launched, and to Willow River State Park, which has eight miles of cross-country ski trails.

It was to the park that my daughter and I headed one perfect January day, first driving through Hudson's neighborhoods. The Victorian frame houses of Third Street still were draped in garlands of evergreen, which the regal homes wore particularly well.

Because Wisconsin was opened to settlers before Minnesota, just across the border, some of the homes are quite old: The Octagon House, now a museum, was built in 1855 for the New York judge and his wife who named the town, and the Jefferson-Day House, now a B&B, was built in 1857. The 1884 Phipps Inn also is on Third Street, which could be called Steeple Row for its many churches.

We ate breakfast at Sunsets, which has big windows and a patio overlooking the St. Croix and Lakefront Park. Then we picked up a pair of pint-size rental skis at Art Doyle's Spoke and Ski.

At Willow River State Park, we skied past Little Falls Lake, up a small hill and into the woods. We didn't make it to the ice-covered Willow Falls, though, because my daughter tired quickly. So I held out a carrot: Hot chocolate at the North Shore Coffee Co., a little espresso bar above the Valley Bookseller.

It came with a pile of whipped cream, a "frog egg"—a green, speckled malted-milk ball—and friendly conversation from the proprietor, who carried our drinks to a thick wooden table in the corner, littered with big, illustrated volumes. We could have stayed there a long time—coffee and coffee-table books being such a pleasant combo—but we wanted to see where the bridge down the street led.

Under the arched "Hudson Wis." sign we walked, onto the old toll bridge to Minnesota that now ends in the middle of the river. On the shore, a raucous gaggle of geese and ducks picked at a huge lump of strange-looking gray stuff and some odd, lettucelike material. We didn't want to get close enough to tell.

It was getting dark, and we only had time to duck into Abigail Page Antiques, named after the first white child born in Hudson. There, we zeroed in on a wall full of dolls, from a 1973 Mod Hair Ken to a exquisite old German doll, dressed in layers of embroidered silk and velvet. The shop, a consortium of 20 dealers, is one of several stores in downtown Hudson that sell antiques, consignment furniture and various bibelots for the home.

We've since visited in other seasons, and now we've got favorite spots. Visit Hudson more than once, and it starts to grow on you.

❸ TRIP TIPS: Hudson

- **Events:** Hot Air Affair, first weekend of February. St. Croix Music and Art Festival, last weekend of July. North Hudson Pepper Festival, mid-August. Christmas tour of homes, weekend before Thanksgiving.
- **Attractions:** The Octagon House, 1004 Third St., is open from May through October and from Thanksgiving to mid-December. (715) 386-2654.
- **Nightlife:** Phipps Center for the Art, (715) 386-5409, overlooks Lakefront Park and schedules concerts and plays year-round.
- **Willow River State Park:** From Second Street, Hudson's main street, turn right on St. Croix Street, which turns into County Road A and leads to the park, six miles from town. On the Friday before the Hot Air Affair, the park offers candelight skiing, and admission is free. Other times, it's $5, $7 for nonresidents. (715) 386-5931.
- **Accommodations:** Phipps Inn, (715) 386-0800, $89–$159; Jefferson-Day House, (715) 386-7111, $89–$159; Grapevine Inn, (715) 386-1989, $89–$129; and Bluebird Cottage, (715) 749-4243, $59–$69.
- **Information:** Hudson Chamber of Commerce, (715) 386-8411 or (800) 657-6775.

Northfield

Two colleges and a famous outlaw

To me, Saturdays in fall should include two things: the smell of burning leaves and, coasting along atop chill autumn gusts, the faint sound of 50,000 football fans cheering.

That's how Saturdays were in the college town where I grew up, and even now, on crisp fall weekends, I subconsciously cock an ear.

I like college towns at any time. But when I found out that in Northfield—a college town twice over—Carleton College would be playing its homecoming game against cross-town rival St. Olaf, I hit the road.

Soon I saw the peaked roof of St. Olaf's Old Main poking over the treetops; then, the Cannon River; then Division Street, where a few dozen beaming parents in sports coats and tasteful sweaters were milling along.

But the town seemed unaware that a game was going on a few blocks away, and the only faint sound wafting out of the stadium toward downtown was a few squeaks from the public-address system.

The joke was on me. In Northfield, gridiron exploits and queen coronations are not that cool, except, maybe, to the friends and relatives of the players; in fact, homecoming candidates have been known to moon the crowd.

Northfield, however, is a lovely place to wander around, game or not, because of its idyllic collegiate atmosphere. St. Olaf's stately and ordered campus is on the west side, Carleton's stone-and-ivy buildings are tucked away on the east, and main street is in between. The town seems to have more than its share of colorful oaks and elms and maples, which, in the fall, put up thick canopies of glowing golds and russets and reds.

The streets between downtown and the Carleton campus are lined with handsome old houses—Queen Anne, Craftsman, Tudor Revival—many rich in architectural detail and lovingly restored.

The 19th century buildings of Division Street are dominated by the Archer House hotel, built in the French Second Empire style in 1877, restored in 1984, and now a repository of lace and handmade quilts and dried-flower bouquets.

The Cannon River flows right behind it; we strolled along the walkway, gazing at the placid water as it flowed toward a concrete wall, then became furious whitewater. Right off the falls is picturesque Bridge Square, lined with a blond-brick post office, the Bridge Square art gallery and the 1868 Scriver Building, now housing the Historical Society Museum.

The museum's main job is to guard the legacy left to the town by Jesse James and his gang in September 1876, when they tried to rob First National Bank and limped away broken, with no money but two dead. The bank clerk and a Swedish immigrant also were shot and died.

But Northfield doesn't dwell in the past for more than a weekend in September, when the famous raid is reenacted. In fact, the town's old motto as the "Home of Cows, Colleges and

Contentment" might be more accurate today if "cappuccino" were substituted for "cows."

Along Division Street, the popular deli Treats Ltd. sells espresso drinks as well as various imported delicacies. Fire Venner has a stock of imported goods from Scandinavia and elsewhere in Europe, and Cherubs Cove is outfitted with antiques and Victoriana.

And yet, Northfield isn't terribly upscale. In fact, it's a pretty good place to visit if you don't have much money. On the same street, there are two used-clothing shops and two stores selling used books. And you can get a room at the Archer House for as little as $35.

And there's something else I relish about college towns: free concerts and recitals, free lectures, free art exhibits. Northfield has loads of them. Also free are visits to Carleton's 450-acre arboretum, or "Arb," along the river, for walks amid its wildflowers and forests in summer and for skiing along its 20 kilometers of groomed trails in winter.

In this town, the sounds of solitude are just as memorable as 50,000 fans cheering.

❂ TRIP TIPS: Northfield

- **Accommodations:** The Archer House, (800) 247-2235 or (507) 645-5661, has 36 rooms, $35–$150.
  Martin Oaks B&B in Dundas, just south of Northfield. Three rooms, $69. (507) 645-4644.
- **Events:** Defeat of Jesse James Days, four-day weekend after Labor Day.
  St. Olaf's internationally known choir, orchestra and band give frequent, free concerts at the college; call (507) 646-3179 for information or an events calendar. The big Christmas festival is held the weekend after Thanksgiving.
  Carleton, in addition to fine-arts performances, has a free midday Friday lecture series. Call the college relations office at 663-4309 for information or a copy of Term Forecast.
- **Historical Society Museum:** Open Tuesdays–Sundays year-round.
- **Information:** Northfield Convention and Visitors Bureau, (507) 645-5604 or (800) 658-2548.

Winnipeg

A prairie town with plenty of joie de vivre

In Winnipeg, I thought I'd died and gone to . . . Europe. I bought gelati—real gelati—in a cafe full of Italians. Ate pierogis next to a table of men arguing in Polish. Was served croissants by a woman who occasionally lapsed into French.

While sightseeing, I came upon a vast stone building, the provincial Legislature, covered with statues and caryatids and sitting in a park like an English lord's manor. On my way to the dim sum houses on the other side of downtown, I passed under a Chinese gate.

This gloriously lumpy melting pot on the flat Canadian prairie is the next best thing to being there. Considering the robustness of the U.S. dollar in Canada and its wimpiness overseas, it may be even better. Throw in the pervasive Manitoba nice—no service with a sneer here—and Winnipeg turns out to be quite a destination.

It's not one big Epcot pavilion, nor is it especially quaint. But you'll know it's not the United States at the border, where the speed limit becomes 100, the radio announces it's a sweltering 28 degrees and signs are printed in English and French. Winnipeg has the largest French Canadian community outside Quebec, a fact best appreciated at patisseries that look transported from the back lanes of Paris.

In the summer, Winnipeg makes up for its long, bone-chilling winters by throwing huge music, theater and cultural festivals. It has wonderful museums, a world-class ballet and shopping that, with an exchange-rate "discount" of up to a third, is delightful.

The city can even be called hip—when I was there, the image of a screaming man in lime-green goggles, advising people to "Fringe Your Face Off" at the Winnipeg Fringe Festival, was on buildings and bus stops everywhere.

Despite all this, residents of this fourth-biggest city in

Canada have an inferiority complex, flogging themselves for being less cosmopolitan than Vancouver, Toronto and Montreal.

"A lot of Winnipeggers do tend to put down Winnipeg, and I don't know why," says Eleanor Mohabir, who came from the Netherlands and is married to a man who emigrated from the Caribbean. "I love it."

Mohabir and her husband, Ron, had walked from their home in the lively Osborne Village neighborhood to The Forks, a renovated shopping, museum and entertainment complex at the juncture of the Red and Assiniboine rivers. They were looking over my shoulder at a list of the summer's festivals, most of which include free performances.

"There's so much to do," she said. "How can we fit it all in?"

During the Fringe Festival, scores of companies perform on nine stages. Folklorama has dozens of pavilions across the city with food, crafts and performances from countries or regions. Smaller festivals overlap: Black-O-Rama, Canada's largest reggae festival; Caripeg Carnival, celebrating Caribbean culture; and street festivals in the neighborhoods that radiate from downtown.

When I visited in July, I headed for Corydon Avenue, known as Little Italy. Earthy aromas of olive oil and garlic floated from a string of outdoor cafes, each jammed with patrons. I had jerk chicken on the rooftop deck of the Sugar Reef, then strolled down the avenue eating pistachio gelati, looking into shop windows and listening to three teen-agers play the bagpipes.

The next day, I drove 20 miles north to Birds Hill Provincial Park, where the Winnipeg Folk Festival, the one best-known on this side of the border, was on full throttle. More than 90 performers were moving among the seven stages in 15- or 30-minute sets; I lunched on Indonesian gado gado and, sprawled on the grass, listened to Claudia Schmidt and ensembles from the Yukon Territory, Ireland and Madagascar.

But I got a dose of Winnipeg at its best Sunday morning at The Forks, on the site of the fur-trading settlement, established in 1734, that became the city. The crowded market was a scene from Europe: crates of fruit, oysters on ice, glass cases of freshly baked focaccia and baguettes. People were strolling along the river, along which water buses run every 20 minutes. A theatrical walking tour would leave later; meanwhile, there was the Manitoba Children's Museum to visit and performers to watch at various "busk stops." On that trip, the weather was fine, and I simply ate and walked my way through Winnipeg. Next time, I'll have to visit the Winnipeg Art Gallery, the Royal Canadian Mint (which makes the gold-tone dollar coins called "Loonies") and the Museum of Man and Nature.

Not that eating is a bad way to spend time in Winnipeg; in fact, I recommend it. With your teeth sinking into a perfect croissant, you can forget, for a moment, that you're still in North America.

⊘ TRIP TIPS: Winnipeg

- **Getting there:** Stop at the Manitoba welcome center for a city map, the current issue of Where Winnipeg and events guides. It's best to exchange money in Canada.

- **Getting around:** Neighborhoods are easy to reach by foot or car, though bikes can be rented at The Forks, $12 for three to six hours.

- **Events:** Le Festival du Voyageur, St. Boniface, 10 days in first half of February.
    International Children's Festival, first week in June.
    Jazz Festival, June.
    Red River Exhibition, 10 days at end of June, beginning of July.
    Fringe Festival, July.
    Winnipeg Folk Festival, usually second weekend in July. For camping information, call (204) 231-0646.
    Taste of Manitoba, mid-July.
    Black-O-Rama, next to last weekend in July.
    Caripeg Festival, August.
    Folklorama, second and third week of August.
    Oktoberfest, 10 days in September.

- **Accommodations:** Reserve far ahead for July and August weekends; if all rooms seem booked, call Tourism Winnipeg for help. Tax is 14 percent; save receipts and you'll be reimbursed at the border.
    The imposing 1913 Hotel Fort Garry, (800) 665-8088, is next to downtown and The Forks, has nice rooms and is surprisingly reasonable: $69–$110 Canadian. Others, all in the $60 range: Norwood, (204) 233-4475; Place Louis Riel, suites, (800) 665-0569; Charterhouse, (204) 942-0101; Carlton, (204) 942-0881.

- **Information:** Tourism Winnipeg, (800) 665-0204.

Appendix

❂ TRIP TIPS: Minnesota State Parks

- **Fees:** Daily passes are $4, annual passes $18.
- **Events:** Open house, first Sunday in June.
  Moms Fish Free, Mother's Day.
  Take a Kid Fishing, second weekend of June, daily fee of $8 waived for a parent with a child under 16.
- **Campsite reservations:** They can be made 90 days in advance by calling The Connection, (612) 922-9000, (800) 246-2267. The reservation fee is $6. Some sites are kept open on a first-come, first-served basis.
- **Lodging reservations:** They can be made a year in advance. In Minnesota, houses within Bear Head Lake, Maplewood, St. Croix and Scenic state parks rent for $90 to $120. Log cabins at Tettegouche rent for $55 to $85, and Itasca has motel rooms, lodge suites, cabins and a clubhouse, renting for $34 to $290.
  For guest houses and cabins, call The Connection. For group centers—Flandrau, Lake Carlos, Lake Shetek, St. Croix, Sibley, Whitewater, Itasca, Myre-Big Island—call individual parks.
- **Candlelight skiing and moonlight snowshoeing:** These events, usually with refreshments and bonfires, are held throughout the winter, along with other events. Call the DNR Information Center for a program guide.
- **Information:** The Minnesota Office of Tourism, (612) 296-5029, (800) 657-3700, will send out park guides, as will the DNR Information Center, which also will suggest parks to visit, (612) 296-6157 or (800) 766-6000 from outstate Minnesota.

❂ TRIP TIPS: Wisconsin state parks

- **Fees:** Daily park fees are $5, $7 for nonresidents. Annual passes are $18, $25 for nonresidents.
- **Events:** Open house (free admission), first Sunday in June. Free fishing weekend first Saturday and Sunday in June.
- **Campsite reservations:** Reservations by mail can be sent starting

167

January 10. Starting Memorial Day, parks take reservations by phone. Reservation fees are $4. Reservation forms can be picked up at each park, or call (800) 432-TRIP to be sent one. Some sites are kept open on a first-come, first-served basis.

• **Disabled-accessible cabins:** Three cabins, at Mirror Lake near Wisconsin Dells, Door County's Potawatomi and Kettle Moraine State Forest Southern Unit, rent for $30. They're very popular, so reserve early by calling (608) 266-2181, TDD: (608) 267-2752.

• **Candlelight skiing:** These events, usually with refreshments and a bonfire, are held at many parks throughout winter. Call (608) 266-2181 for a list of ski dates and other events.

• **Information:** For a Wisconsin park visitor's guide and a Summer Recreation Guide, call (800) 432-TRIP.

Index